Prais

'I'm not sure if I should be happy or offended that Tahira and her beau's favourite make-out spot was in the cinema watching my movies (which kind of explains the strange smiles both of them have on their faces whenever they meet me). This wonderful book is full of many such gems that will make you laugh as much as I did. More love to Tahira.' **Shah Rukh Khan**

'Downright honest and delightful with its buoyant wit, this is an all-candles-ablaze celebration of the female mind.' **Twinkle Khanna**

The 12 Commandments of
Being a Woman

The 12 Commandments of Being a Woman

Tahira Kashyap Khurrana

JUGGERNAUT BOOKS
C-I-128, First Floor, Sangam Vihar, Near Holi Chowk,
New Delhi 110080, India

First published by Juggernaut Books 2020

10 9 8 7 6 5 4 3 2 1

P-ISBN: 9789353451219
E-ISBN: 9789353451226

Typeset in Adobe Caslon Pro by R. Ajith Kumar, Noida

Printed at Thomson Press India Ltd

To all women, irrespective of their age, caste and creed.
And to the men who are intrigued by women and their
every issue, desire and need.

'The most alluring thing a woman can have is confidence.'
Beyoncé

Contents

Contents

1

**Don't wait for your fairy tale from dusk to dawn
An ugly duckling can take forever to become a swan**

School was my first home. It was where I had all my meals except dinner, where I studied, played and completed my homework in the one and a half hours I had to wait for Mama to finish teaching at the senior school – we juniors would finish at 2.30 p.m. but classes for the seniors went on till four. School was also the place I would relieve myself – do the big job – and that's why I call it my first home.

My mother, who was the head of the English department for the senior school, was obsessed with Shakespeare, Wordsworth, Tolstoy and other literary gods, which is why between the ages of seven and ten I was a little freak who recited their works and came first in elocution contests, while not understanding a word of what I was reciting.

To make things worse, I was turned into an exhibit at every goddamn dinner and lunch get-together. This is a truly cowardly adult device: when the conversation begins to dry up, they make the kid the sacrificial goat, turning Basant Panchami lunch into Eid.

Over the years I tried every trick to get out of it. I said I was shy or feeling unwell. Sometimes I locked myself in the loo and sometimes I gave in immediately hoping they would feel bad. But nothing ever worked. The adults showed no mercy, and thereafter I ignored all the moral science lectures I got from them because of these double standards.

At 10 . . .

I was no longer the cute little prodigy with pigtails and a perfect memory. In fact, I was a far cry from being cute. I had thick glasses, with a power of minus 3, my school tunic almost reached my ankles and my socks came up to my thighs, which meant I was a far cry from being cool, too.

As we approached puberty, this feeling of being a freak seeped into other areas of my life. We had a pair of gorgeous twins in our class, truly divas. They and a tall, blonde sardarni got all the attention from the boys, and I became the little runner who would relay chits and love letters for them. I blamed my mother's presence in school, and not my geeky looks, for the lack of attention from boys.

As I returned home every afternoon riding pillion on my mother's two-wheeler, I would sing, 'I am all alone, all alone, with no one to love me,' from the Disney movie *Ugly Duckling*. Mama would laugh, but I was serious.

The song soon became part of my ritual on the morning ride to school too, so by the time we had to sing the national anthem at the school assembly I had already warmed up my vocal cords.

Then came a day when Mama had had enough of my whining. She stopped her scooter, turned around to look at me and said, 'You know that the ugly duckling became a swan eventually, don't you? That's what's going to happen to you, too.'

A tiny part of me wanted to believe her. And so life moved on.

One day I was chewing gum in class. Of course, this was a big no-no in school. I don't know what came over the teacher, but instead of scolding me and asking me to spit out the gum, she slapped me. Super hard.

What happened next was a scene out of a movie. The slap was so hard, its angle, the timing and the distance between the dustbin and me was such that the gum flew out of my mouth at 100 frames per second and landed plonk in the bin. My classmates looked ready to break into applause. As for me? I had never felt more like a freak.

The teacher certainly shook something in me – her slap may even have (briefly) rewired my brain because I ended up coming first in the on-the-spot writing competition that she angrily announced to stop the sniggers in the classroom.

At the end of the school day, as I carried my first prize to Mama's scooter, I saw the twins opening another love letter. 'I am all alone, all alone,' I sang, my voice up by several decibels.

At 13...

I still hadn't turned into a swan. By now many girls in my class had got their periods, but not me. I kept a jealous tab on who had got it, and even lied to a senior about this sore subject. The discussion went something like this: 'Hey, have you tried the new sanitary pad? It sticks directly to your panties. You don't need a string like for the old one. How about you? Which one do you use?' I had no idea what she was talking about but nodded knowingly, saying, 'Same, same. The old one.'

That year my music teacher chose me to be part of a play. I was thrilled. I loved acting and it was always a high to get picked for a school play. Then I learnt that I was being cast as Ramu Kaka, an old man, even though our school was coed.

I had enthusiastically coached a friend to audition for Ramu Kaka's role. The teacher must have noticed this and, of course, considered my lovely flat chest an added advantage. Pissed, I reached home and told my folks, but surprise, surprise, they were happy!

Only Mama understood my plight. She said, 'You are a late bloomer, like me; it will happen.' But seeing her fabulous chest, I knew she was lying.

At 14 ...

There were about eighty girls in my batch, and I was the only goddamn fourteen-year-old who hadn't got her periods and was stuck in a camisole, rather a vest that I could share with the boys of my class (mine was only missing the VIP tag). Effing Mama had lied!

I was becoming unforgiving towards her. Perhaps hitting your teens does that to you. I started looking for reasons to hate her. And there it was. My mother doesn't have time to look after me!

Both my parents were working. They treated their jobs as if *The Tribune* wouldn't get published if Papa missed one day at work and the school would shut down if Mama missed teaching her kids – her actual kids – at school.

A genetic oddball, I began to feel I must have been adopted (you would have thought that too if you had seen my mother's figure). From the hole in my sock to my faded uniform to the boring tiffin (or no tiffin at times) to walking alone to an empty home after school to making my own snack and having no one to play with – I had many grudges against my parents, but held them only against my mother.

This was probably a form of conditioning. If anything went wrong in the family or with the weather, the economy, the neighbours, the traffic, the cat or even the cows who lazed on the roads of Chandigarh, only one person was to be blamed – the mother or, more specifically, my mother.

And to top it all, there was this colossal crushing-your-spirits kind of problem – the no-show of the boobs and periods. Life was so, so, so unfair.

Every day I would complain to my best friend and

we would find solace in eating our juniors' tiffins. I was also eating a large quantity of dates because an aunty had said, 'Khajur garam hote hain,' and that they help in ovulation and periods. My face was soon full of pimples. And periods? Well, for me they only meant something at the end of a sentence.

I started to mimic how girls behaved when they were on their periods. That you got them only once a month clearly hadn't registered with me.

So every once in a while I would hold my tummy and wince in pain. I got the attention and sympathetic looks I craved. 'Poor thing, she has to bear the pain; periods are tough.' I thought I was acting rather well, but a friend once nearly caught me out.

'You just had your periods a week ago and the pain is back?'

'Uhhh . . . perhaps this is just stomach pain,' I said. Phew, that was close.

The girls in my year had moved to playing FLAMES, writing their names alongside the names of the boys they liked, striking out common letters and ending up on Friendship, Love, Adorable, Marriage, Enemy or Sex depending on the number of letters left. In my head, of course, I wasn't even

9

eligible for such a game. I had to first prove to myself that I was really a girl.

I tried stuffing Mama's hankies into my camisole and taping them on to my chest, but they wouldn't hold. The tapes in those days weren't strong enough. I tried wearing my mother's bra in the bathroom, and that didn't just leave me sad, but completely crushed. I was convinced I would never be able to reach her towering heights. Ms Towering Heights teaching *Wuthering Heights* at school. Lame one.

While I was dealing with these insurmountable problems, my parents decided that I should get braces. So now I had a metallic smile with weird bands in my mouth, along with pimples on my face and a flat chest. And don't forget, I already had spectacles.

In 1996, Gandhiji frames were a style statement, and I guess they still are. But kids didn't get how fashionable my father and I were to wear matching spectacles. Oddly, it looked good on him. And on me? Well, nothing was working for me at that age.

The more I heard tormenting news like 'oh, this one has got her periods' and 'that one is wearing training bras', the more convinced I became that I was not normal.

Moreover, I thought the world and my mathematics teacher were conspiring against me and rubbing salt into my wounds as we spent the entire year solving mensuration sums. Even though my best friend tried to tell me that we were studying mathematical mensuration while girls get biological menstruation, it brought me no comfort.

My chemistry teacher was perhaps the ringleader, as he kept harping on about the periodic table. One day he had the audacity to say, 'The sevens rows of the table are called periods.' And I swear he said it while looking at me. 'Itna direct? No period-ic shit, seedha periods!'

I was aghast. Nothing was making sense to me. I think along with my periods many of my grey cells were also lying dormant.

One day I decided that whining and self-pity weren't going to help. I told my mother that I needed to see a gynaecologist as I was not a girl, and that the doctor needed to check my vagina and confirm that it was normal. When my mother, disbelievingly, said no, I threw a major tantrum.

Mama was losing it. She said, 'I gave birth to you and I know you are normal.' I convinced her that my vagina was not like the one I saw in my biology book. There was something definitely wrong down there. She told me to show her. And that's when I had a meltdown. My poor mother had to take half a day off from school for our visit to the gynaecologist.

I lay there on the stretcher-like bed, my skinny legs hesitantly sprawled. I felt like running out but held my ground and my breath.

'What is the complaint?' the doctor asked, her head under the white sheet that covered my legs. In that dark space it was just her eyes and my vagina and her torch. She was expecting a serious chat, even though we couldn't see her face.

She repeated the question sternly. I couldn't speak. My mother mustered up the courage to blurt out, 'She . . . she doesn't feel she is normal.' I could tell she was feeling totally ridiculous but wanted to show she was on my team, at least to the world.

The doctor popped her head out from under the sheet and gave us an incredulous look, doubting both my mother's and my sanity. She rolled her eyes, dived back under the sheet and said, 'There is nothing wrong. She is absolutely fine.'

I told her that her expert eye had missed a spot, and that I seemed to have – not wanting to get into the gory details – all kinds of folds down there, big and small. So weird.

The doctor held my hand and said firmly, 'That's how it looks. Trust me, I see so many in a day. Yours is nothing unique. Kindly get down and wear your shoes.' And looking all judgemental, she said to my mother, 'Try talking to her. That will help more than these rounds to the doctor.'

So now I had been declared crazy? As we came down the stairs my mother didn't say a word, but I could sense her anger in every step. We reached her silver Kinetic Honda.

She self-started the scooter and said, 'We could have saved money if you had shown it to me! What were you doing in class when you were being taught the reproductive system? Or haven't you been taught yet?' She was still trying to get the scooter started. I wished it would work as Mama hated kick-starting. 'I have been taught in class,' I mumbled.

Finally, the engine started. Thank god. I sat behind Mama. She adjusted her rear-view mirror and asked me, 'Then?' I looked right at her and said, 'But mine doesn't match the diagram.'

She turned her head towards me murderously, and I had the audacity to say, 'Mama, let's go to another doctor.' Behind her helmet's visor, her eyes turned into a fiery ninja's – they were red, the veins ready to pop. 'Shut up!' she said.

We whizzed down the empty roads of Chandigarh in the high heat of summer. Every two to three kilometres we passed by carts laden with watermelons. The size of them made me think of my other grievances.

At 15 . . .

One day, early into the tenth grade, a classmate and I got into a fight. He threw my books out of our second-floor class window and I got so upset that I flung his spare sports uniform out of the window, just as the bell went off for the sports period (ugh . . . there was that horrible word again).

Now, this guy's English wasn't that great. He went running to the staffroom where my mother was sitting with five other teachers and screamed, 'Ma'am, your daughter took off my pants.'

Mama was livid and called for me. Before I could say anything, she slapped me hard in front of the entire staffroom. Without uttering a word, I just walked away.

When I met her near the scooter at the end of the

school day (this was transition time for me – from Ma'am she became Mama), she was still furious. 'How could you touch him? How could you take off his pants?'

I was shocked. 'Is that what he said?' She nodded. 'I threw his spare pants out of the window, not the ones he was wearing, for heaven's sake.' Instead of feeling apologetic, she broke into a huge laugh. Now I was burning, quite literally. Mama nonchalantly started the scooter and we made our way home.

As soon as I got off the scooter, I felt something wet. I turned around to see what I had been waiting to experience my entire life. The biggest, happiest daag-acche-hain stain on my tunic. Slaps have truly been iconic in my life. Thappad se sach mein darr nahin lagta, sahib.

2

**Put doubts about yourself to rest
Believe in yourself – it's simply the best**

As you may have guessed, I was a bit of an achiever in junior school. I stood first in all the elocution competitions and was always cast as the lead character in our school plays. And, of course, I earned a prefect badge for these glittering extracurricular activities.

Then, at age eleven came grade six and senior school. Senior school was a whole different beast. It was run differently, too. In junior school, there was a headmistress to whom the schoolteachers reported. Senior school – from sixth to twelfth grade – was run by the vice principal and the principal. I was sure I was going to rock it just like I had in junior school. But I was wrong.

I hadn't accounted for the politics between teachers. For if there are some pros of having your mother as a teacher (subsidized school fees being a big one), then there are lot of cons as well. Some teachers were nice to me because of my mother, but others weren't, especially those who didn't like her.

And somehow this co-curricular prefect wasn't chosen for any intra-school competitions, let alone interschool ones. I was denied all opportunities.

Initially I couldn't understand what was happening. My confidence began to drop, but my mother kept pushing me. 'You must prepare, you must participate,' she would tell me. I would argue with her, saying, 'I am not allowed to participate, let alone win!'

And so from sixth to ninth grade (as I struggled with not getting my periods and having no boobs), I added one more thing to my list of woes and another reason for my growing anger against my mother.

There came a time when I knew I wasn't going to be selected even before I stepped in front of the teachers for the try-outs. The chances of never making it were becoming stronger. It irritated me that my mother refused to get it. She would force me to stand with my prepared speech or poem. 'Keep trying, never give up' was all she said. I don't think she knew what it meant to be rejected all the time, every time.

Then came grade ten. The dreaded year we had

been warned about since we were in grade two. Those momentous board exams, the marks of which would determine our future. Trust me, I haven't given a single interview where anyone has asked me about my board exams. Of course, what you become and how your character and skills develop do depend on the schools and colleges you attend, but this undue pressure isn't justified.

Like several others, the pressure of being in grade ten had haunted me since I was a kid. And now here I was, facing the precipice. No more wasting time. It was study, study, study. So when the school announced that there was to be an interschool competition in Delhi, no student came forward. Who do you think seized the opportunity? Yes, it was me.

Two of us were being sent by the school. I was participating in the English category and my partner was chosen for the Hindi segment. The day before we were to leave for Delhi, our vice principal called us to hear our prepared speeches. My partner killed it. She was really good and had learnt her piece by heart.

Me? Well . . . I was the same person who had been beaten down repeatedly for the last five years. I hadn't taken part in any of the school competitions, and here I was being sent not just to another school, but another city!

I gulped, my hands were sweaty, my knees buckled, and I stammered and fumbled my way through the piece. The vice principal nodded quietly, unable to give me even a word of encouragement, let alone the appreciation she gave my partner.

We went to Delhi in the Shatabdi train with our English teacher Ms Jyotsna. It's remarkable how a few moments with a positive person and a few words of motivation can light a fire in someone.

I saw my partner rehearse again and again despite knowing the speech by heart. Ms Jyotsna pushed me to do the same, and I could sense that she had faith in me. Perhaps all she wanted was for me not to forget my piece and fumble on stage, and I didn't want to prove her wrong either. And so I, too, rehearsed my piece for the three and a half hours of the train ride, without taking a minute's break.

My practice didn't end on the way to the hostel where we were put up, it didn't end during my dinner and it didn't end the next morning. It was twenty-four hours of constant rehearsal.

We arrived at Sawant Singh School, the venue of the competition. Thirty-three schools were participating. Two kids from each school. I was competing against sixty-six students! I had imagined fifteen students, twenty max. This was way out of my league. But I didn't stop rehearsing.

All the teams were really good, and had prepared well. They went on stage one after the other, while I waited in the wings for my turn. And then it was time. I stood on the dais. The auditorium was huge and filled with participants and teachers and other students.

I fixed my mic. I gulped, my hands were sweaty, my knees buckled, but I didn't fumble. It was as if I was where I had always wanted, and was meant, to be. The junior school co-curricular prefect resurfaced, and how!

I got so excited that I concluded the speech with a violent twirl of my hands and a quote by Napoleon, just like a little French revolutionary. Everyone loved it and clapped hard. I stepped down and sat next to Ms Jyotsna, who gave me a look of pride and a warm squeeze. And, honestly, that was enough for me.

Seeing my teacher's and the audience's response, I thought I would get a participation certificate. After what seemed like an endless wait, the results were announced. As the dignitaries called out the names of the kids who had won participation certificates, I waited to hear mine. But it wasn't announced. I felt really bad. Despite being rejected for five years, I still wasn't used to rejection.

I clapped along with the rest of the auditorium. Then they announced the name of the student who came third. I hoped against hope that I would make it, but my name was still not called out. Well, I wasn't really expecting it, I thought to myself, now feeling really deflated. The name of the student who had come second was announced. I continued clapping mechanically.

Then they announced the name of the student who had stood first among the sixty-six kids. Tahira Kashyap. I clapped. Ms Jyotnsa shook me. 'Whom are you clapping for? It's you, it's you!' I looked at her unbelievingly. I couldn't fathom what had happened.

In a daze, I didn't stop clapping even as I headed towards the stage to get my prize. People must have wondered what an overconfident girl I was, clapping for myself, but what they didn't realize was that these hands were used to clapping for others and they couldn't break the habit suddenly. I was on the stage. I had at most expected a certificate, but here I was with the biggest trophy.

A small embarrassing detail. After I won, I was numb for a while. And then it hit me. I went berserk with happiness. As we headed back to the hostel room, I couldn't contain my excitement and peed in my pants.

But that's what winning after five long years does to you. I am just so thankful to all those years of being rejected. The doused fire once reignited is nothing short of a blaze.

3

**Everyone has their own love story
Don't feel bad if yours isn't full of glory**

At seventeen, my friends and I didn't know what falling in love really meant, though we were obsessed with the idea. We took male attention for granted – if you were an average-looking seventeen-year-old in Chandigarh, it was constant. It must be admitted, we weren't always kind to the boys. Every time I got the standard card and a chocolate from an admirer, I would accept the chocolate and shamelessly return the card.

The boys were ingenious. They hid their tokens of love in all sorts of places. I'd find a chocolate or a card or some stupid stuffed toy lying next to my bag or in my friend's scooter carrier or jammed under my car's wipers.

Thank god they spared the girls' washroom. Extracting chocolate from places like under the sink

29

and behind the dustbin would have been gross, but not taking it would have been impossible. We were constantly hungry, you see. And treats, no matter who they were from, were always welcome.

My friends Divya and Prerna and I were preparing to become doctors. I mean, that was the intention. So we took tuitions to prepare for our PMT (premedical test).

Prerna and I went to the same tuition classes. In every class we shortlisted one boy as a prospective crush. In the physics class we both had a crush on a boy who was skinny but cute. It was a class of seventy, and we didn't know his name. Prerna and I were too careful (and snooty) to ask someone or to actually talk to any of the boys.

We were living at a time and in a place where inquiring after a boy would have cost us our reputation. We would have been labelled as easy. It's obnoxious, I know. It was the other way round when it came to us. The entire class knew our names. It's not that we were gorgeous, but that's how it was.

In the film *Minority Report*, Tom Cruise just has to swipe his fingers in the air for information to pop up on a virtual screen. Ha! That was nothing compared to my batchmates who were a mix of Cruise and Arnold Schwarzenegger from *The Terminator*.

As soon as they locked sight of their target, not only would they know the girl's name, but her entire biodata would pop up in front of their retinas – house number, sector, phone number and also her status, whether it was single, committed or complicated.

This is one department in which I concede defeat to boys. Our skills were nowhere close to theirs. So we two Nancy Drews spent the entire year trying to figure out the name of that cute boy we liked with zero success.

Meanwhile, boys could dig out unknown details like the astrologer Maharishi Bhrigu, and know everything there was to know about the forefathers of the girl and the Google Maps location of her ancestral house before Partition, and nobody would judge them! I am convinced Google Maps was launched in the heads of the horny teenage boys of Chandigarh seven years before it actually made it to our phones in 2008! On the other hand, if a girl were to simply ask the name of a boy then she was easy or madly in love or wanted to get him beaten up!

Those Chandigarh boys

The gedi route was perhaps the best example of messed-up boy–girl relations in small-town India. What is gedi route? It was a unique Chandigarh phenomenon in which girls and boys chased each other mindlessly from sector 10 to sector 11 in their cars and scooters. The boys would be playing loud gabru music and pursuing the girls, and I would be lying if I said some girls didn't enjoy it.

Sector 10 was the closest market to my home and unfortunately lay at the heart of the gedi route. I had to cross it every time I drove to school and later college.

We didn't know what to say to our parents. We never discussed it with them because we didn't want to be dissuaded from leading normal teenage lives. For all you know, they could have banned us from driving around the city or taking tuitions in the evening. But, thankfully, none of the creepy teenage boys that followed us stuck around for long, except for a stalker I had at school who was finally scared away by my boy and his pals when we were in college.

Many Bollywood and Punjabi songs boast about this culture in their lyrics. It wasn't just the gedi route where we were followed. Boys, groups of boys, would be waiting for us after tuition class. At the end of every class we planned and mapped our exit and tried to fool the enemies. So when Narendra Modi came up with the surgical strikes in 2016, the planning wasn't new to us. We had been doing it ever since we hit puberty, some of us even before that.

We had two Kinetic Hondas and as per plan, we would go in two different directions and then meet at one common point. So much thinking went into this on a daily basis that had the same brain cells been used by the boys and us to understand the dynamics of chemical equations, at least some of us would have become doctors and justified spending our parents' money.

One winter evening, when the days are short and the nights set in pretty early, we began our usual exit operation after physics class. The boys followed and we tried to evade them. The race was interesting as we managed to leave two out of the four bikes behind. Before Hrithik Roshan knew how to do this in *Dhoom 2*, we had become experts. All that was left for us to learn was Ajay Devgn's balancing act on two vehicles.

So now two bikes were behind Divya and me, and god knows how many behind Prerna. Divya tried to make her way through the tiny streets and gullies, but they continued to follow us. We had run out of escape routes and were left with no choice but to enter my sector. Determined not to reveal my address to the boys, we stepped on to someone else's porch and pretended it was ours. Once we stopped the bikes, they usually left.

One day I would really like to know their side of the story. There must be a reason for behaving like jerks. However, that night one bike followed us straight to our fake house. Divya and I were hiding behind the gate, and we saw the rider take off his helmet. We were sweating even though it was ten degrees outside, clinging to each other.

We looked at the man, and then at each other in confusion. It was Divya's father!

We felt relieved. Safe, but also violated. How can parents start following us? But looking at the positive side, we were happy that he would know we were doing nothing to provoke the boys to follow us. Yup, justification mode again. But then we started wondering if this was the first time Divya's father had followed us or if he had done it before. Had we ever given a wrong signal to the boys? By the end of it, we didn't know what to feel; we were being followed by both parties without our consent. Yet again, the female species in the small city was left confused.

Thank god times are changing, but Kabir Singh playing to the gallery and people appreciating it sends shivers down my spine. I found Shahid Kapoor very hot in the film, but what is glorified in it is something most of us dread in real life.

So the entire year went by with us calling our crush Coolio and leaving it at that. It was a really cheesy name, I know, but we found his gel-spiked hair and his cute specs, skinny frame and dimples really cool.

One day our test papers were being handed out. Prerna and I were all ears. This was our golden chance of discovering our boy's name. As soon as sir called out the name Abhishek, the paper was passed to Coolio.

Hmm ... Abhishek. We made a mental note. We told Divya about this Abhishek boy and how cool he was on his Yamaha bike with the extra lights. Unable to contain her curiosity, Divya decided to bunk her tuition one evening to come to ours and take a look at him. She was the gutsiest of the three of us so perhaps she would even talk to him and open the door for us.

Divya arrived on her father's Vespa on the big day. We waved to her excitedly and she looked eager, too. Good-looking boys were a rarity and Coolio had been heavily built up in her head. Without switching off the engine, Divya looked in his direction and said, 'Yeh hai?'

We both nodded in unison.

With a look of disdain, she turned her scooter around and said, 'It's better I attend my class.'

'What?' Prerna and I cried out in surprise. 'She doesn't like him?' We dismissed it as lack of taste.

The year was coming to an end, and so was our physics class. Not a word was exchanged with Coolio, though I received around two dozen chocolates and cards from the other boys in the class.

One day my father declared that we had to go for a family dinner. 'Chandigarh is a small town. We didn't go for their house-warming party, so we all have to go for this dinner. He is specially organizing it for us.'

'Who is he?' I asked.

'He is a very renowned and respected astrologer.'

I quickly picked up the cordless phone. It had turned from white to grey and the numbers on the keys were faded – a sure sign that you have a teenager at home. I punched in Prerna's phone number, wishing I had a similar memory for equations.

'Tell your parents that if they allow you to attend this dinner with me then we will get to know our future and the money we are spending on classes and admission forms can be saved. Once you come, we'll tell my parents that we aren't in a mood to go, and we can chill the entire night.' We could hang out and make crank calls, one of the great joys of pre cell phone teenage life.

Prerna loved the idea. She took permission from her parents and came over. But our plan didn't go according to script. When we told my parents that we weren't in the mood to go, they insisted we come along. 'It's a family thing and we have also promised Prerna's parents that she will talk to astrologer uncle,' my mother said. Prerna looked at me in horror, but I was helpless.

The one saving grace in this mess was that our host had two kids. The elder one was apparently our age, so we'd have someone to talk with.

We reached their house and were seated in their living room. I looked around, taking in the room. There on the wall opposite me hung a big family portrait of the Raichands, with the mother and father sitting on chairs and the two sons standing behind them. One of the sons was Coolio!

I squealed, 'Prerna . . . Coolio!' At that exact moment, Prerna saw him walk into the room to greet us, and squeaked, 'OMG, it's him!' I said, 'Where are you looking? He is . . .' and there he was right in front of us.

This was a typical filmy Teja moment from *Andaz Apna Apna*. Prerna and I were grinning. We eagerly followed Coolio into another room (for the kids to hang out) and that's when we discovered this wasn't the Raichand family of *Kabhi Khushi Kabhie Gham* (same vibe though, trust me), these were the D'Souzas. On the wall of this room was another picture of the four of them, this time with the mom in a frock, the father wearing suspenders and the sons sporting bow ties.

Of course, they weren't the D'Souzas or the Raichands. They were the Khurranas. And he wasn't Abhishek, he was ... well, why would you be interested. He was just a boy who was melting our hearts because after my father sang (he is a trained classical singer), this boy started crooning 'Bade acche lagte hain', which had Prerna and me swooning. That one dinner cost our parents years of crazy phone bills and, a decade later, marriage banquet hall charges.

Within a few months of that dinner, I was seeing my boy. The attraction between us was high. We mostly had movie dates at a single-screen theatre called Nirman in sector 32. That year we watched *Asoka* fourteen times. Kareena Kapoor's 'San sana na na nan' rang in our ears as we clung to each other.

The movie that beat *Aśoka*'s record for us was *Lajja*, which we watched nineteen times. We knew the storyline of *Aśoka*, as my boy was a big SRK fan, and we watched it properly at least once. But when it comes to *Lajja* I draw a blank, as we spent all those hours . . . well, discussing chemistry equations.

It took us six months to get to first base. But it stopped there, despite my boy's every attempt to take us to second base. I really did test his patience.

I was nineteen and still not confident about my breasts. Even though they were decent-sized, watching *Baywatch* had set standards that I could only dream of. By now some clever company, seeing the distress of women, had brought padded bras to India.

I bought mine from a humble store in sector 35 that Divya and Prerna had introduced me to. It was called Fancy Store, but it was not very fancy as they had limited styles and sizes and we invariably needed to force our assets into the bras that came closest to our size.

Emboldened by my bra, we did go to second base, but it was much harder than I had imagined, because we never had a place to ourselves. There was a disastrous trip to a hill station, and one scary time when he came home and my father nearly caught us in the act.

With not many options left for two horny teenagers, we gave in to the inevitable. We made our friend drive my boyfriend's silver Santro Xing around town while we had a great time in the back seat.

Of course, we made sure he had turned the rearview mirror away from us and a couple of times we noticed him turning up the volume of the music, too. 'Rhythm divine' and 'Hero' by Enrique Iglesias would make me swoon and the car would swerve just on cue. Yet, despite our chemistry and us getting closer, I never stopped dreaming of getting triple D cups.

We were having a gala time. Then something happened that changed everything. Now my boy and I were united by our mutual attraction. But we had a lot else in common as well, especially our love for theatre and public speaking.

This often resulted in us being pitted against each other at college competitions. He represented DAV College, sector 10, and I was at GGDSD College, sector 32. So in a way we were lovers who were often rivals.

We were both gearing up for the annual youth festival where we were acting in our respective college's plays. Rehearsals took hours every day and we weren't able to see much of each other.

The big day came. The competition was being held at Khalsa College, sector 26. The college building was buzzing with the energy of all the teams getting ready. The classrooms had been turned into make-up rooms.

We hadn't seen each other for a while. Being ultra-competitive, we hadn't even discussed the plots of our plays with each other. And today we would be seeing each other on stage.

Now you have to imagine this in slow motion. We are both in the wings of the stage. My performance is right before his. We look at each other. I am dressed up as a transsexual and he as a bald man.

His play is about bald guys, so backstage was bobbing with bald heads. Beefy baldies, thin baldies, tall baldies, short baldies, baldies with specs, braces and pimples. And among this sea of bald boys, there is a flat-headed one with a skinny body, bushy brows and a dimple which has my heart. I cheered madly from the side as they began their performance.

My look was as dramatic as my boy's. I was

wearing a garish glittery suit that could blind anyone. At five feet, eight and a half inches, I really suited the part, and don't think I required much make-up. All those years of 'Oh, you look just like your father' were coming to my aid that day. On stage I spoke in a Bachchan-type heavy bass voice, and I could see my boy smiling in the wings.

As we cheered each other on, our pupils dilated, we got goosebumps and our knees went weak. That day, my friends, we fell in love with each other. True and weird love.

I have heard many unusual love stories about the moment a couple fell in love. None have come close to being this odd. I had to become a transsexual and he had to be bald for us to really fall for each other.

His team won and ours came third. Still light-headed from the feeling of love, we didn't cool our hormones off in the theatre, but went to the lake instead where he, as always, sang a song for me. 'Bade acche lagte hain . . . yeh nadiya'. My glittery suit sparkled in the water as did his shiny head in the winter sun.

4

**Small towns have many laws
It's hard to break them and be a rebel
with a cause**

It's hard to be a rebel, especially in a small town like Chandigarh. But having the raging hormones of a twenty-year-old, and with my parents heading out of town for an overnight trip, you can feel my need to break the rules, right?

I gave them the usual excuse of how much Prerna, Divya and I needed to study for the upcoming exams, trying to convince them to let us have a sleepover that night.

They looked at me sceptically. I admitted, 'Okay, we want to have some girlie fun, too.' They smiled, underestimating their daughter's plan, or perhaps they knew better than me what bad behaviour I was capable of.

After much pleading, the other two sets of parents gave their permission as well and, yippee, our plan was in motion. The three of us gathered at our front door, bidding adieu to my parents who perhaps had their own naughty plans. Then we started plotting how to get our respective boyfriends into the house.

The first obstacle was sixty-year-old Mrs Gill, my most vigilant neighbour. So whatever we had to do would have to be done when villains mostly strike – at night.

We made a lot of preparations that day. We got cold drinks; sadly the boys didn't drink alcohol and we didn't want to push our luck, so Fanta and Coca-Cola it was. We bought chips. Now the last thing we needed to arrange was a movie.

We girls decided to celebrate our chromosomal conglomeration of Xs and rent an XXX film. I don't think the boys would have appreciated it because that's what they did the whole day anyway, but for us it was a novelty.

Now the question was how we would get a CD and what we would say to the VCD guy. The video rental shop was in sector 11, and I couldn't go and ask for the CD as the shopkeeper would recognize me. I was a regular customer and usually picked up cartoons from him which I loved (don't laugh). He would get the shock of his life. 'Baby went directly from pink movies to blue.'

I didn't want him to get any ideas, so the deed would have to be done by either Divya or Prerna. But neither of them was willing to go. Even our daredevil Divya didn't want to raise eyebrows. Such are the taboos in a small town.

So we devised a ploy. One of the girls would cover herself in Mama's dupatta, revealing only the eyes and the nose. Mummified girls on scooters on the roads of Chandigarh were a common sight.

But we forgot that we were using my car. And there was no need for a girl to cover up in a car, as the only reason girls acted like they were on *Mummy Returns* was to protect themselves from the sun and reduce their chances of not making it to the advertisements for Fair & Lovely.

With a mummified Prerna in the car, we drove nervously at a snail's pace. What were we thinking? A girl covered up with a dupatta in a car that was moving at the speed of thirty to forty kilometres an hour? It was the opposite of inconspicuous. We were asking for turned heads and craned necks.

We parked the car across the road from the shop and Prerna left for the mission. That's when Divya and I realized our folly. Both of us swore we wouldn't say a word to Prerna, but the thought had struck our warrior, too. She came back running, saying, 'Why the f**k did we come in a car?' Oops. 'Listen, it's going to get dark, our boys will be here soon. Let's just go. I feel stupid wearing this dupatta.'

She did look stupid in it. The dupatta belonged to my mother who is five foot nine inches tall and liked them to be longer than usual. Prerna was five foot two. The dupatta fell around her like a tent. Her look was screaming for attention, much against our plan.

Now that we had got here, we didn't want to return empty-handed. So we pushed her, and finally Prerna agreed. Divya and I were sweating in the car watching the conversation between her and the shopkeeper. The latter's face looked grim at one point. I thought he was going to call the police. Divya said, 'Why would he? Wouldn't he get caught, too?' She had a point.

The next instant we saw the shopkeeper roaring with laughter. Prerna lost the plot at this point. Not only did she unmummify herself, but she screamed at him, her face now completely uncovered.

And, to my surprise, the six-foot guy shut up and handed her a CD.

Prerna came back angry and victorious. I wanted to give her a chest bump. I was so bloody proud of my friend. Divya said, 'He knows you now,' to which Prerna replied, 'Good, perhaps next time he will think twice before he says "Ladkiyan toh sirf ek hi rang ki filmein dekhti hai, tumhein badi aag lagi hui hai" to some other girl.'

The three of us laughed. Two hours of elaborate plotting had just gone to waste, or maybe it hadn't.

So now we had the entire set-up ready. We were exactly twenty-six hours away from my parents' return. The party was about to begin. It was 7 p.m. when we got home, already pitch-dark. Winters do that – shorten the days and extend the nights. Just what we wanted!

We went to the terrace, the part that had the Sintex water tanks and a clothes line. The clothes were fluttering like capes behind our three silhouettes, just like the Dark Knight, except these Batmen were women waiting for their Batboys.

We kept a close watch on Mrs Gill, who had just finished dinner and was watching *Kahaani Ghar Ghar Kii* followed by *Kyunki Saas Bhi Kabhi Bahu Thi*, after which she would start her nightly walk. This meant that our mission of sneaking in the boys had to start right then. We called them and on cue they drove in on three bikes, their 'dhoom machale' moment.

The boys parked their bikes in my driveway and came up. We lived on the first floor. The ground floor belonged to my father's brother and was vacant as he lived in the States (from where he used to send me an exotic and irresistible product, Nutella, that won me attention in school for days).

The stairs overlooked Mrs Gill's bedroom, and as they walked up to our floor, the boys could see her watching her serials. Just then a commercial break came on, and she got up to use the washroom. The boys immediately fell to their knees and began to crawl up the stairs.

We all had our hearts in our mouths. Mrs Gill came back rather quickly, and glanced briefly from her window into my house. The boys froze and shut their eyes tight, hoping it was all going to go away. 'How the hell will closing your eyes help?' I muttered under my breath.

Thankfully, Mrs Gill's daughter-in-law came into the room with her medicines. Mrs Gill began to pop her multicoloured pills and that's when Smriti Irani came back on screen, with Mihir being resurrected for the fifth time.

Mihir's existence defied or perhaps redefined the concept of a phoenix. Not only did he rise from the ashes multiple times, but he did so with a different face each time. Plastic surgery did wonders on TV; it did not just change your face completely but it also altered your height, complexion, shoe size and eye colour. Perhaps that's what misled all the women who have given so much business to cosmetologists and plastic surgeons.

The boys were finally in the house and we celebrated with Coke and chips. We told them about the precious CD we got, but none of them were interested in watching it. The idea of community viewing creeped them out, and by now us, too.

Giving up on the idea, we started to gravitate towards the corners we had allocated to each couple. My boy came close to me, sending a shiver down my spine. This was the first time he was going to spend the night at my place. No sooner did I feel his hand under my T-shirt than I screamed out, 'F**k,' loud enough for it to echo through the whole house.

'Sorry, did I hurt you?' asked my startled boy. 'No, but Mrs Gill surely will!' I had just realized it was time for her walk and she would see the three bikes parked in my driveway. She knew my parents were out of town and I was home with my girlfriends, so she would suspect something was up.

The six of us panicked. Now before Mihir vanished again and Tulsi became hysterical, we had to get the bikes out. But where could we take them?

That's when Divya's boyfriend suggested that the bikes could be left in the sector 17 parking lot and we could come back home in my car.

Gosh, another challenging proposition. The song 'Ab tumhare hawaale watan saathiyon' started playing in my head. My two friends looked at me helplessly. Neither of them could drive. They would have to be good soldiers and defend the home front from our neighbour across the border fence.

So the boys rolled their bikes out of the porch as kick-starting them would have shifted Mrs Gill's attention from Tulsi and she would have slipped into Karamchand mode. While they were walking their bikes in the lane, I tagged behind in my golden Zen.

Luckily we stayed in sector 3, which was synonymous with retired people. So all the old people were indoors and no one was in the lane to watch this strange parade. Finally we reached sector 17. The boys parked their bikes, and we all got inside my car.

As we headed back, the girls called. 'Mrs Gill is walking in the garden, you guys can't come back.'

Damn! So much for when the cat is away, the mice will play. We had to spend the next two hours at the junction of my sector – the weather was too romantic for Mrs Gill who decided to chill in the garden with her husband after her walk.

My Sony Ericsson phone finally beeped at 11 p.m. The girls called to say that the lights had finally gone off at Mrs Gill's house. We were drained of all energy, which was evident in the lame 'yay' I got from the boys.

We reached home and the boys had to painfully crawl up the stairs again. This was one time I wish Baba Ramdev had had some influence on them and inspired them to be more agile. All of us were famished. After a dinner of cheese toasts, everyone was too tired to raise a finger, let alone make out.

We all crashed out. It was going to be a super short night. We had to get up at 4.30 in the morning as at 5 a.m. the milkman would come to Mrs Gill's house. She would take the milk from him herself every day, and would then on be in and out of the house constantly, walking her schoolgoing grandson out and supervising Kalawati's sweeping and cleaning of the driveway. She was painfully active, which meant I would have to drive the boys to sector

17 and come back and park the car at its regular spot before Mrs Gill woke up. And we did just that.

My parents returned at 10 a.m. and looked at the three of us, pale and tired. 'You seem to have studied all night,' they said, tongue-in-cheek. Perhaps they hadn't underestimated their daughter, but had only known her too well.

Epilogue

But I just had to prove my parents wrong. And in a few weeks, we got another opportunity. This time Divya and I were spending the night at Prerna's house and we decided we weren't wasting it over boys. A late but good realization.

We bought a few bottles of cheap vodka, the only thing we could afford. While Divya was having her drinks like a 'lady', Prerna and I were downing shots. 'We did it! This is rebellion at its peak,' I said.

And then Prerna started puking. I got up to help her, only to take a quick detour to her washroom, where I stayed for the next three hours vomiting my guts out.

The girls had to eventually drag me out. My hands and feet were cold. I was delirious. For some reason, the only words ringing in my head were 'cheap vodka se cheap thrills hi milengi'.

In my haze I think I saw Prerna barf from her balcony, which landed below in her neighbour's balcony. And I think I saw Divya, the only sane one, managing frantic phone calls from the neighbour saying, 'My friend is sick . . . nahin nahin . . . alcohol toh bilkul touch nahin kiya, dawaai ki smell hogi.' At one point her tone changed, 'Aap keh rahe ho hum acchi ladkiyan nahin hain, hum jhooth bol rahein hain?'

Once she went on the offensive, the calls stopped. I was feeling extremely cold now, but I managed a congratulatory smile. Friends can make you do that, even though it felt like my last smile before dying. Poor Prerna and Divya got very stressed about my condition and rubbed my hands and feet through the night.

Later when I expressed my gratitude to them, Prerna said, 'It wasn't love. I didn't want a freaking dead body in my house.' So much for love, and so much for rebellion.

5

**If you don't want your sanity to go for a toss
You should skip the wedding chaos**

My boy proposed to me. And I said yes. It was time for the Great Punjabi Wedding. First up was our roka, a Punjabi ceremony conducted before the engagement or the wedding.

As the name suggests, it means to stop. We were now booked for each other. Nobody could consider us for a romantic alliance and neither could we look elsewhere. We weren't looking but this was pressure. I think the medicine Roko, used to stop loose motions, gets its name from this ceremony.

On the day of our roka we were too awkward and shy to sit together in front of our parents. My boy and I were such geeks that while pursuing postgraduation in the same class, we didn't share a bench even for a day. Our friend Sukriti, who is an art director, had to later photoshop the only photo we clicked together during the ceremony where we were sitting two feet apart. And that became our Facebook update.

My boy and I had entered the stop-and-wait stage of our relationship, but it was go, go, go in the Kashyap family. The wedding was in eight months, but, as you know, everyone gets super excited about a big fat Punjabi wedding. By everyone I mean my family. And by big fat I do not mean the festivities of the Raichand khandaan or *Made in Heaven*. Our wedding was a middle-class affair, but had a lot of heart and craziness.

Things got especially crazy in the last month. My masi came down from Pune to help my parents with the preparations, so did my nani and my younger cousin Gudiya (don't judge me, every Punjabi family has a Raju, Pinky, Gudiya, Sonu, etc.) from Jalandhar.

No matter how busy people are in their lives, everyone in Punjab makes time for a wedding. Delivering a baby can wait, divorce papers can be filed a month later, the electricity bill can stay unpaid even if it results in the power being disconnected. But going for a wedding is of utmost importance.

Most close relatives apply for a month-long leave from work or school. Schools are extremely adjusting and understanding. Authorities will think twice before granting sick leave when a child has chickenpox or precautionary leave from work during times like the coronavirus epidemic. But a wedding, now that's a month-long emergency and you will always get leave for it. That's how small towns work.

So my relatives were stationed at our house for a month. And it was particularly stressful for Chhotu Masi (don't start judging again, every family has a Chhotu as well), for she was shocked at my size.

I had lost a lot of weight (I am not very proud of this and will come to it later in the book) because I was dieting and working out like a maniac. Along with losing kilos I had lost inches and had become a 34B (that too with a padded bra), which didn't go down well with her.

Every day Masi would give me suggestions on how to increase my breast size. It turned into a mission for her. You see, breast size hasn't been just my obsession. The entire planet has been fascinated by it. For some their breasts are too big, for others they are not big enough. It's an eternal – and for most of us, a very invisible – struggle.

Concerned about me, Masi did an online search on silicones, and trashed the idea as soon as she saw the obnoxious size of Pamela Anderson's breasts. I tried explaining to her that there were many sizes and we can choose according to our taste, but undergoing a procedure twenty days before the wedding wasn't a viable idea. Moreover, we weren't sure anyone in Chandigarh at the time knew how to do it. 'Cancer-shancer ho gaya toh!' she said worriedly, which makes me laugh in retrospect today!

Masi didn't give up hope, though. She used to take me for chocolate facials. I never understood what the deal with them was. The only difference seemed to be that they were fancy and cost one hundred and fifty rupees more than regular facials. While I had my luxe face pack on, I overheard her asking the parlour lady about ways to increase breast size.

The parlour lady stared at Masi. 'Isn't this enough already?'

'It's not for me, it's for . . . uhh . . . Kareena,' stammered Masi.

I rolled my eyes under the cotton wool that was covering them. Yeah right, Masi. In a town where we have names like Harmeet, Sandeep, Pinky, Vishal and Rocky, you had to come up with Kareena? When I was waiting to make the payment I saw that the only poster at the entrance was of Kareena Kapoor.

As we were leaving, the parlour lady smirked at me and said, 'Thank you, Kareenaji, I mean, Tahiraji.' I was livid. As soon as we got into the car I started screaming at Masi. She was silent for two minutes and I thought to myself, 'She seems upset, finally this will stop.'

As we drove home, Masi got busy on her Samsung Galaxy 3 (the era of smartphones had just begun). She was speaking to some colonel's wife, Mrs Dixit, from Pune and, to my shock, she was asking her for breast enhancement advice.

Furious, I immediately hit the brakes, risking being hit by the truck behind us. I gestured to Masi to hang up as she muttered about my poor driving skills. We were about to break into a full-blown fight when my father called and told me to pick up three dozen rasgullas.

I was the kind of bride who was involved in everything. The list of recent calls and numbers stored on my BlackBerry that month looked liked this: Raju Halwaiwala, Bittu Jewellers, Radhe Photographers, Sweety Laddoos, Jyoti Home Beautician, Kaka Tent, Vicky Small Caterer, Vijay Blood Test Sector 9 (for my grandmother – we had to monitor her blood sugar regularly), Kamla Massage (for the ladies in the house to get massages).

This also meant that the blushing bride was getting into a lot of fights. When Kaka Tentwala presented me with tablecloths, half of which were pink and the other half blue, I screamed, 'It's not a birthday party for five-year-old twins!' So the next day he put out dark purple ones with gold bow-tie ribbons around the chairs. Some battles cannot be won.

I was on to my next fight the day after with the aunty from Kanta Suits, as her measurements couldn't keep pace with my weight loss. Along with running eight kilometres every day, these daily battles contributed a lot to the weight and mind loss.

Masi, in the meantime, had not given up. She discussed women's assets and how important they were for a successful marriage with my mother, Nani and Mrs Gill (yes, that Mrs Gill) over chai and rusks. The next moment I saw Mama and Masi whipping up something in the kitchen under Nani's supervision. They made me sit and eat some concoction that had imli in it. Apparently it would work like magic. Of course, it didn't lead to an increase in breast size, but it did lead to increased tooth sensitivity and cost me many dentist trips in the middle of all the wedding chaos.

I gave up. And I thought so would the rest of them. But a week later I received a courier which said 'Urgent' on it. Getting urgent couriers in those days wasn't that common, so I thought this would be important.

I took it to my father who was in the living room enjoying his moment of rest with evening tea and Bourbon biscuits. Masi, Nani and Mama were also in the room. Kamla was massaging Nani's shoulders. Hardevji, our family electrician, was busy fixing a tube light. Most people have family doctors and physicians, but we have family plumbers and electricians who have been working for us for the past twenty years and are not allowed to leave without having tea or food.

Hardevji was standing on a stool in a corner with the screwdriver in his mouth, when my father opened the courier. In the box were two tubs of cream. He picked up one of them and read out the label, '100 per cent guaranteed. Massage clockwise and anticlockwise for ten minutes daily to increase the size of breasts'.

My father could read an entire page without registering what's written, and as far as he was concerned he was reading washing machine guidelines. I was so mortified that I wished the floor would open up and consume me à la Sita maiyya.

Instead of being embarrassed, Masi said, 'Shukar hai, it has come. Mrs Dixit sent it; her daughter-in-law had ordered four bottles. Here, Tahira, this is for you.'

Hardevji choked on the screwdriver – thank god he didn't swallow it – but carried on with his work. Kamla went pale as she saw the image of the breasts, luckily placed on the side of the tub not visible to Papa. She continued massaging Nani as if she hadn't seen anything at all, Papa went back to sipping tea as if someone else had read what he had and Mama excused herself on the pretext of preparing saag.

The only people who were excited were Nani and Masi. I looked at them in disbelief. My reputation had gone for a toss. Now along with the length of the tube light he was fixing, Hardevji also knew the size of my breasts.

Would Masi ever give up? Cheerfully she nattered on. 'Her daughter-in-law got married five years ago. These bottles are from the US. She used two tubs and these two are about to expire. That's why she was generous enough to send them. But nevertheless let's just start from today.' I couldn't believe my ears.

In protest, I stopped taking her for household errands and my beauty parlour visits. My next trip to the parlour was for waxing. I told the lady I needed the regular waxing for arms and legs and a simple bikini wax, nothing fancy. I liked being well maintained, but I didn't want to feel like a bare chicken. In small towns beauticians get super excited about weddings. She said 'no problemo' as if she regularly visited Spain. I asked her where she had learnt the phrase, and she proudly said she had also learnt 'hasta la vista' as she was looking for a groom who would take her to Canada.

I didn't have the heart to tell her that she didn't need to know Spanish in order to go to Canada. I should have told her to hone her Punjabi instead, since there is a mini Punjab in British Columbia and Toronto. My arms and legs were done, and now it was time for the bikini wax. Before I could stop her, she took the centre route and waxed the life out of me.

I screamed in agony and wished Masi was there

so I could hold her hand. With her around maybe the beautician wouldn't have gone this far. With tears in my eyes, I asked, 'Why did you do that?'

She said, 'For your honeymoon, Didi. Give your husband a surprise.'

'I don't like the surprise myself! I said bikini, not Brazilian,' I shrieked. 'Oho, ki farak painda hai,' she said matter-of-factly. 'Dono hi b se shuru hote hain.'

I felt like killing her. I got up and said, 'Stop right now,' only to see that I had become a distant cousin of the shom shom shom shom sha sha–singing Amrish Puri from *Tahalka* with his penchant for weird hairstyles, except mine wasn't on the head. I was sporting a barren Gaza strip with flora and fauna on either side. Not a great look. So I spent the next thirty minutes screaming and shouting as the beautician finished the job. Somehow I knew this was Masi's way of making me miss her. I came back home feeling and looking like a fifth grader.

~

The wedding festivities started the next day. First up was my sangeet and engagement ceremony. I was wearing a lehenga with a short choli, flaunting my waistline and abs while inviting the ire of my paternal grandfather. Most of the relatives missed the exchange of rings as they were too busy discussing the length of my choli, but I am so grateful that my immediate family didn't judge or try to dissuade me.

In fact Masi, the lone warrior, had gone to Kanta Suits and got an extra pair of cups installed in my choli. Well, as long as she was happy, I was happy.

The wedding was the next day. We spent the entire night of the wedding touching the feet of hundreds of uncles and aunties. Before they could congratulate me, I would dive at their feet. I saw more footwear than faces that day.

My father and brother-in-law had bribed the pandit so that our ceremony was done and dusted in one hour as opposed to the 'taaron ki chaaon mein' marriages, where the pheras don't happen till 4 a.m. and leave you so tired that no amount of turmeric milk can help with the groom's gravity-defying erections. But our wedding was different. It ended early and so everyone ate food on time and left in time, too.

The night finally came to an end. My parents, after crying hundreds of buckets, were ready to leave. Everyone had left, expect my boy's parents and brother and my parents, Masi, her son Simran and Nani.

It was a weird moment. The two families had decided that the newly-weds should stay the night at the hotel, but no one had booked the room. It was so embarrassing; I was standing in the lobby like a Christmas tree with nowhere to go. My boy was confused (as he still is).

My parents came to my rescue. My father said he would quickly book a room. Papa took my cousin by the arm and said, 'Come, Simran, let's fix this.' We all sat down with some coffee and waited.

There was an awkward silence as we all knew what the room was being booked for. Indians are strange. For most of their lives they tell their daughters to be wary of boys and their monstrous dicks, and then one night they want you to tie a ribbon on it. I don't know why everyone makes such a fuss about the first night, as if before the wedding couples only make plans to visit Vaishno Devi or the Golden Temple.

After what seemed like eternity, my father and Simran were back with the biggest grins on their faces. Papa proudly declared, 'The room has been arranged,' and gave me a smile.

I had my 'my papa strongest' moment. You can always count on your father, I thought, feeling a surge of emotion. How I was going to miss him!

'It's all set, no need to worry, it's a beautiful room, beta. Simran and I checked everything and have a surprise for you.'

We bid goodbye to everyone. Only Aparshakti, my boy's brother, and his friend escorted us to our room. We walked along the corridors. I was a one-woman Indian band with my swishing lehenga, rattling bangles, jangling kaliras and rackety payals. The only thing missing was a trumpet.

Aparshakti had the key to the room. I was eagerly waiting for the surprise so that for the rest of my life I could taunt my husband about the amazing things my parents did for me. We opened the door. And before I could take in the scene, Aparshakti cracked up like a gleeful Ravana and immediately called up his best friend in America.

My father and brother had booked a room with two single beds. Not only were the beds separated by a distance of four feet, but they had also filled up the space between them with all the flowers and bouquets we had received, creating a Berlin wall of sorts. Perhaps hidden underneath those sweet-smelling flowers were tripwires and a bed of nails. I couldn't put it past my father.

I didn't find the scene as funny as my brother-in-law did. Forget one-upping my boy, now he would dine on this story for the rest of his life, and so would his brother and his best friend.

The moral of the story: it's best to elope and save yourself the harassment of a wedding. On a side note, Chhotu Masi still hoards all kinds of creams, not just for boobs, and often well past their expiry dates!

6

They come in all shapes and sizes and have
all kinds of flaws
But you simply must love your in-laws

I was twenty-five, and after the roka I went back to my job as the programming head of BIG 92.7 FM in Jalandhar, feeling excited about the wedding and the marriage ahead, while my boy went back to Mumbai, where he was working with MTV.

It seemed like a piece of cake. After all, I had dated my boy for seven years, and our parents knew each other. But my spirits were dampened when I was given a series of diktats by my friend Meghna.

Meghna had been married for a year and was an expert in the intricate details of a Punjabi marriage. Her advice wasn't about sex or our relationship, but something more pivotal. 'You need to start calling your mother-in-law "Mummy",' she said.

Now I had tried this earlier but the transition from Aunty to Mummy was as difficult as asking Kejriwal to give up his muffler, that too in winter. I picked up the phone in the middle of managing a dispute between my programming and sales team and said, 'Hello, Aun . . . mmyy.'

She corrected me, 'Beta, not Ammi, say Mummy.' I felt like an idiot.

How do you adopt another set of parents at the age of twenty-five and call them by the names you only associate with your parents? The pressure kicked in when my fiancé effortlessly transitioned into calling my parents 'Mummy' and 'Papa'. It was as if he had always had them in his life. How? Bloody hell, I needed to up my game.

Each time I got off a call with Aunty . . . I mean, Mummy, I had to follow it up with a call to Meghna who dissected it. 'How long did the call last?' she would ask. 'Did you speak with her yesterday as well?' 'How does that even matter?' I would say. 'Her son doesn't even call her twice a week. Why are you making me call her twice a day!' She believed it was important to build the dynamics of our relationship. If it was a two-minute call, I was instructed to take it up to twenty.

Meg stressed me out even more when she asked me what bed sheets I was buying. We are not giving any dowry, I told her. The in-laws, too, had made it clear that they did not want anything. But there are unsaid expectations, she said.

Bed sheets? Really? Well, she was experienced in these matters. So I filled my suitcase with new bed sheets, towels and blankets. I felt like a refugee, hoarding things before being banished from my country and heading off to unknown lands. But Meg insisted, and my nervous parents went along with her weird suggestions.

I was their only child, after all. They had no experience as far as weddings were concerned and did not want any screw-ups. Typical BPS – Bride's Parents Syndrome! A part of me felt like screaming out that our relationship wasn't dependent on towels and bed sheets. If, god forbid, something bad were to happen between the two of us, would I be saying, 'And don't forget we gave you VIP towels and Bombay Dyeing bedsheets.' And what would he say? 'Yeah . . . I completely forgot . . . you know what, I think we should make this marriage work.'

The length of my chats with my mother-in-law progressed from two to twenty and then thirty minutes. We talked about everything, and were only short of discussing Newton's laws and why E is equal to mc^2. Our relationship did become better. It had never been bad but these conversations deepened our bond, although they also had a very embarrassing aftermath.

While linen and cutlery were being accumulated at my end, she, too, was up to something. And for this something special she made a quick trip to Delhi.

I thought she was going to buy me heavy-duty jewellery. I started practising how to say no nicely. 'Nahin, Mummy, this is too much.' 'Arre, iski kya zaroorat thi.' 'Yeh toh main bilkul nahin accept kar sakti.'

Once she returned to Chandigarh, my mother-in-law called me home. I drove over, rehearsing the responses in my head.

She gave me a warm hug and asked me to take a seat. She had a packet next to her and told me that she had gone all the way to Delhi to get it for me. 'It's important I give it to you now so that you can wear it on your wedding day.' I started saying, 'Nahin, Mumm–'

Before I could complete my sentence, I saw a pair of bright-red lacy bra and panties, another set of the same colour in satin and one lonely thong! I was speechless. I accepted the lingerie awkwardly, but I could sense she was expecting a response.

'It's very bright,' I said weakly. She looked at me waiting for a more enthusiastic response. 'Uhhh . . . nice, too.' Still not enough. 'Uhhh . . . and lacy.' The pressure was building. Finally I said, 'Thongs are my favourite.'

'Mujhe pata tha; they are my choice, too.' She beamed proudly.

Really? I thought to myself. I feel uncomfortable just getting a wedgie, and here I was vouching for a thong which practically rides up your ass!

The one time I wore a thong bought from Fancy Store I couldn't keep my hands off my bum. For once I empathized with the Indian male who can't keep his hand off his crotch and is absolutely unapologetic about scratching it at any given place and time.

So there I was bonding with my mother-in-law over our love for pinnis and fetish for thongs! The nightmare didn't end as she wanted me to try the bra and let her know how it fit. I didn't have the heart to tell her, 'Aun . . . mmy much against your hopes, your to-be daughter-in-law isn't a 38D.'

I had come a long way from my ninth grade troubles, but the journey to 38D seemed eternal. I felt this revelation would have been more devastating for her. So I went into the washroom and squealed in excitement, 'It fits so well, Aun . . . mmy!'

Don't have sex for the first time
in a remote place

What do you do when you get the licence to have sex? After all, that's what marriage, or for that matter even roka, means. The dorks that we were, we planned to go for it only after the family agreed to our marriage. I am sharing the load of being a dork with him, but it was my idea (and I absolutely do not judge people who choose otherwise). The boy, deprived for six long years, was excited. He planned a trip to Kasauli and booked a place for us to stay.

I was shitting bricks, but I was excited, too. As we drove up to the hill station, we began to romanticize the epic moment we were going to share.

We experienced the first glitch at Gyani da Dhaba, my family's usual pit stop for aloo parathas and paneer naans. The sardarji began to give us suspicious looks as he had always seen me with my parents.

As we paid the bill, I said 'The paneer naan

was very nice, my fiancé loved it.' As a middle-class Indian girl it's my duty to explain myself to every second person, just as it is a random person's right to question every girl.

Of course, my boy didn't feel he owed anyone an explanation, a feeling I was envious of. But for now it was *my fiancé* liked the food, *my fiancé* will pay the parking ticket, *my fiancé* wants to use your washroom. Gyaniji's wife said 'Yes, *your fiancé* just bought condoms along with Fatafat.'

The look I gave my boy as we sat in the car should have killed him, but it didn't as he, the privileged Indian male, felt no guilt. He tried to cajole me by saying, 'Baby, we are 100 kilometres from home, Gyaniji or his wife don't have your folks' numbers, and he will not leave his shop to travel for two hours just to tell on us. Lastly, our folks know we are headed to the hills; they know what's happening.'

I screamed at his logic which annoyingly made sense. He was right about everything except that my parents were expecting this.

My boy put on 'Hero' by my favourite Enrique

Iglesias to calm me down. I loved Enrique but listening to his music always confused me as I didn't know which version of the singer to fantasize about, the one with or without the mole.

We finally reached the guest house. I was seeing spies and accusing eyes everywhere. Luckily there were no other parked vehicles. The place was beautiful and totally secluded. It didn't receive any signal for radio or mobiles and neither was there a TV.

We looked at each other and grinned. This is what we wanted. No intrusions, no speculations, no onlookers, no guilt trip. By now our hormones were raging. We went to our room – a neat bed with clean sheets, two small chairs and a table for tea and pakoras (food is always playing on my mind), a small balcony with pots of bougainvillea and a view of the mountains.

The clouds that we could see from our room brought a smile to our faces. Everything was perfect.

The first kiss and hug were awkward. Of

course, we had kissed and hugged before and gone to second base, but today the intention was to get to the final act and it was making us jumpy.

We were nearing the big moment, and I don't know if it was because of my theatre background but I began to make awful faces. My boy stopped and asked if I was okay. I nodded casually and said, 'Of course, of course.'

I told myself, 'Control yourself, make a pleasant face.' He gathered himself and tried to go for it again. This time I managed to smile, which slowly turned into a constipated look. When I couldn't pretend any more, I let out a scream.

He shushed me and asked what was wrong. It was painful, and Gyaniji being in my thoughts wasn't helping. He tried to calm me down and asked if I really wanted to go ahead. I nodded vigorously. Now the pressure was on me.

On the third attempt I tried to relax myself. But as soon as he tried again, I came up with a McDonald's combo offer – screaming, making awful faces and wincing. The poor guy jumped off me.

I apologized. He said he was feeling like a criminal. There was an eerie silence. Everything that had seemed so perfect to us moments ago now felt like agony. There was no mobile connection so we couldn't pretend to talk to someone else, no TV for distraction, no radio, no people. Just the two of us in that room and, of course, the chai and pakoras, the slurping and munching of which were the only sounds filling the awkward silence.

During the period that we were engaged, I managed to smoothen the bumpy road that a mother-in-law and daughter-in-law usually walk on, with a little help from Meghna. But the thing about in-laws is that there's always a disaster looming around the corner.

Take our first night in my boy's home post the wedding. The house was beautiful and cosy, the welcome was warm. My heart was fuzzy with love. We played the traditional game of finding rings in a bowl full of water, milk and rose petals, the significance of which I still don't know.

Then it was time to untie the threads that had been tied on our wrists earlier in the day. I undid his easily but mine had a million knots, which I felt was again a ploy by my family to obstruct my sex life. My boy kept at it until most of his family was ready to call it a night and his father said, 'Just use the goddamn scissors.' I liked him already.

So off we went to his room. It was a bachelor pad. I assumed his parents had not bothered to do it up as we were supposed to live in Mumbai. But I don't think they anticipated the problems of a tall daughter-in-law as the bed or sofa-cum-bed or whatever it was couldn't accommodate this Goldilocks!

My legs dangled off the bed, so I curled into a porcupine position, which was back-breaking. I asked my boy how he managed.

He said he slept diagonally when he was on his own. 'So where do your parents expect me to sleep?' He said, 'My parents used to fit easily so they must have assumed . . .' I wasn't happy with his response. 'Yeah . . . sure . . . how the hell are we supposed to fit on this bed when you at five feet nine inches are the tallest in your family and I, half an inch shorter than you, am the shortest in mine.'

I have proof of this hanging on my wall at home. It's a family picture of the Kashyaps and Khurranas. Everyone seems to have stood in ascending order of height, god alone knows how, so you can actually trace a line over us, with the Khurranas starting at five feet and going up to the Kashyaps ending above six.

Your assumption that the night did not lead to any sex is right. So the next morning when I went downstairs with swollen eyes and my mother-in-law gave me a look that said 'It must have been one helluva night', I really wanted to say 'Oh yes, hellish it was.'

Now the custom was for the daughter-in-law to cook something in the kitchen for everyone. Thankfully, we had already had the conversation where my mother-in-law asked me, 'Beta, what all can you make?' and I replied, 'Practically nothing.' So there were no undue expectations from me. All she wanted me to do was put sugar in the kheer that was being prepared on the gas stove and give it a stir. It is a tradition which we tweaked a bit.

Again, I need to brief you about the family I

was born into. We are not very religious. We live by certain philosophies but never went to the temple much. I often visited the gurdwara because of Nani. I remember one time I went to a temple. I was twelve and a friend of mine took me when we were in Jalandhar for our summer break. I was fascinated by the life-size deities. The pandit walked over to give us water and we cupped our hands to receive it. My friend drank the water, and I washed my hands with it.

I presumed that the water was given so we could wash our hands before receiving some prasad. My friend gulped. Panditji was appalled. I was kicked out and banished from that temple forever. I felt bad, but I had not known any better.

So that was me, ignorant when it came to rituals and religion. I entered the Khurranas' kitchen which has a small mandir. I remembered the incident in the temple and told myself not to screw up here.

There were a few silver bowls with glistening white sugar cubes kept on the countertop below the wall-mounted mandir. I thought, 'This is fancy.' Sugar cubes were served in hotels and only refined white sugar was found in homes. These people clearly had fine taste.

So I took a sugar cube and was about to put it into the kheer when the house help Phulwati, a product of K serials, started screaming, 'Bahu wants to poison the entire family.'

My mother-in-law came in running. Phulwati was hysterical. 'Komolika, Auntyji, Komolika,' she said, referring to the melodramatic antagonist of a serial the two were avid watchers of. My mother-in-law was just short of turning her head thrice to look at me as was common in those soaps, but instead she said, 'Beta, this is camphor, not sugar cubes.'

I could have died of embarrassment. Phulwati was still suspicious of me and doubted my intentions. I wanted to tell her I hadn't signed the marriage registration papers yet, and so wouldn't gain anything by killing everyone, including myself.

Mummy crossly told Phulwati to stop watching so many serials. That day I earned one hater – Phulwati – and one supporter – my mother-in-law – for life. I heaved a sigh of relief. In the days to come I would often mess with Phulwati by circling around her teacup with camphor balls in my hand.

And yet my ordeals as a newly-wed were not over. I remember a chat between my boy's grandfather, his mother and me where I was told about how the ladies in the family changed their name once they were married. My mother-in-law, Poonam, was Lalita before she got married. She started listing all the women in the family who got married and changed their names.

I nearly choked. For twenty-five years of my life I had been Tahira. I was ready to give up on this marriage but I couldn't be named Sita for my Ram. I have no problem with the name Sita, but Tahira is good enough for me. Now anyone from the right/left/centre/up and down wings shouldn't get any ideas. Thankfully, my in-laws got over the disappointment at this break in tradition.

In fact, unlike most Indian homes, things have always been rather good with them. The secret to our relationship lies in the fact that we are constantly shocking each other and keeping things fresh. From being gifted thongs to finding a condom in my in-laws' dresser, Mummy has kept me on my toes. She, on the other hand, has had to deal with a giraffe-like bahu who is capable of accidentally poisoning them and once walked in on my five-year-old daughter engrossed in sponge painting with a padded push-up bra! You see, we like to keep it simple.

7

**You need patience and courage
Not to kill each other right after marriage**

After our wedding, and that first near-disastrous stay with the in-laws, my boy and I headed to Mumbai. Our first marital home was a humble 1.5 BHK in the suburbs where my bachelor husband lived with his loyal man Friday Santosh.

My dedicated husband had taken only five days off from work for the wedding. His contribution to the wedding was arriving in Chandigarh and at the venue, and before that locking up the Mumbai flat since Santosh had been given ten days off.

Two jobs. That's all. One, to be present at his own wedding, and two, to lock up the house. How tough is that? He did manage the first, but the second? Well . . . when I opened the door I was welcomed by more than a few dozen beings.

Nope, I don't mean neighbours or friends welcoming me with garlands and confetti. Instead, I had more than fifty, perhaps a hundred, cockroaches moving towards me with their creepy antennas. The look in their eyes, or whatever they have, seemed to say, 'Welcome to paradise.'

I looked at my newly married husband in horror. Is this how he lived in Mumbai? But he seemed equally shocked and was jumping and screaming like me. We waded through the pool of roaches trying to figure out what had happened. And that's when I learnt exactly how efficient my husband was. Wives learn such lessons much later into the marriage; for me it took less than a week.

My boy had to lock up the house before leaving for the wedding. But what he didn't know was that one doesn't need to shut down the refrigerator loaded with food. The fridge was full of arsenal and the cockroaches were having a gala time, like teenagers when their parents are out of town.

When we opened the fridge, the look on their faces was gleeful and totally disgusting. I slammed the door shut and stormed into the small living area, where the roaches were completely unfazed by my angry presence.

I think animals in Mumbai, be it cats, rodents or these roaches, are pretty chilled. On our late-night tapri feasts of Bournvita shots and idli (a staple for strugglers and suburban people), I have seen rats the size of puppies who aren't scared of the cats who in turn aren't scared of the dogs. It's like they have an agreement to live in peace owing to the scarcity of space, something we humans haven't figured out yet.

The roaches were witness to the first argument of the newly married couple. It was not a pretty sight. I was furious, screaming and nearly in tears. I was also stuck in this hellhole as we didn't have the money to casually check into a hotel. My neighbours were kind enough to offer us tea and sympathy but couldn't do much else. We tried calling pest control but they said they could only make it the next morning.

So this is how I spent the first night in my new home with my brand-new husband. I went to bed with my back towards him, my mouth tightly closed and my index finger plugging my ear so that the tiny crawlies couldn't explore my oesophagus or Eustachian tubes.

The next day, after getting the home cleaned, I found the crockery drawer had two plates, two spoons, two glasses and two bowls. What a cute welcome, I thought, just like Goldilocks, only to be proved wrong when Santosh returned and claimed the second set. So yeah ... the romantic two spoons and two plates were for my husband and his loyal man Friday. This Goldilocks had to buy her own plate and cutlery.

I soon settled into Palm Springs, the building we lived in. I found the neighbours friendly and nice and the complex had a squash court. It was a cosy year, maybe too cosy.

One day as I was heading to play squash, an aunty from the society came up to me and said, 'Aww, kitni cute behen–bhai ki jodi hai tumhari.' I was shocked and also heartbroken. It turns out she was convinced that we were siblings and had said so to everyone else in the building.

Now don't get me wrong here, we always have been excited about each other but, as mentioned earlier, we were never fans of public displays of affection.

We are around the same height. He is only half an inch taller which goes unnoticed if I wear a shoe with a thick sole, not even heels. We also wore spectacles that had very similar frames. I was a minus five and he was a minus three, the only upside being that two minuses make a plus. That was downright cheesy.

I am not exaggerating when I say we were both helpless without our spectacles. We would grope for our glasses first thing in the morning, one of the many characteristics we had in common. I can't remember the number of times we have knocked off each other's glasses during make-out sessions.

But being nearly blind did have its advantages. If we felt a hotel room or a place wasn't very atmospheric, we just took our spectacles off Rajinikanth-style, and voila, we turned into Amitabh Bachchan and Rakhee swooning over each other in a foggy room à la 'Kabhi kabhie mere dil mein'.

Finding each other without wearing spectacles was our biggest form of foreplay. Our hands fumbling about would land at the most inappropriately appropriate places. It was far more titillating. See, finally a plus to this minus situation.

Lenses were tiring, so at home and in the society we would wear our glasses. We both played squash and were equally good. But I am not sure how any of these things indicated we were siblings.

I had no idea that's how people saw us. Is that how comfortable we had become over the years? What if they had spotted us on the rare occasion we romantically held hands? Had we introduced the holier-than-thou society aunties to incest before Jamie and Cersei from *Game of Thrones*?

Yuck! I had to address this issue, and the only way to do it was to go all out. Regular conversation would have been too boring for this masaledaar neighbour aunty, so I waited till Karva Chauth to strike.

I dragged my boy to the terrace where the rest of the ladies and their husbands were cursing the moon for their 200 gram weight loss. And there in front of everyone, under the full moon, my husband and I shared our first public kiss. It was like getting married all over again.

Aunty gasped and was about to do a Simran, only her SRK wasn't looking at her and she couldn't fake the fall. Meanwhile, all the other aunties' eyes were fixed on her, questioning her sanity. Locked in my husband's arms, I could hear people murmur, 'Aww . . . kitni cute romantic jodi hai.'

8

Know this is true
Fad diets will never come to your rescue

By the time I left my job at Big FM, I was easily seventy to seventy-two kilos. It was a sedentary job and my appetite wasn't helping. When people took cigarette breaks I had two huge steel glasses of carrot and beetroot juice and ate peanuts and chana the entire day. This was separate from my meals.

My plan was to quit my job, spend some time preparing for the wedding and be with the family. I'd then move to Mumbai and find a job, but I had very little idea of what I wanted to do next. With lots of free time on my hands, I had a new mission – to lose weight before the big day.

I started working out like a maniac. When my body got used to one-hour aerobic classes, I pushed myself further and started doing two classes in a day. The weight did drop but reached a plateau. I was obsessed with hitting the fifties on my weighing scale.

I had grown up with mostly petite girls whose weight was in the forties or fifties and had always felt like a big moose next to them. I conveniently forgot that I was much taller than my classmates and friends and it is not healthy for someone my height to weigh that little.

When two hours didn't feel good enough, I began running by Sukhna Lake. I started with four kilometres and progressed to eight, going up to twelve kilometres on a good day. So on most days I was doing two hours of aerobics along with eight kilometres of running.

I lost weight, and my mind, too. But I still hadn't hit my target weight. I decided to go on a crash diet without consulting a dietician. I went online and soon learnt the calorie count of practically every food item from rajma, rice and vegetables to even a clove of garlic. I was obsessed.

At one point I was having one toast for breakfast, a bowl of chickpeas for lunch, diet namkeen and tea in the evening and bowls and bowls of dal for dinner. A week before the wedding I weighed fifty-nine kilos. I had made the impossible possible, and I am not proud of it.

The weight loss didn't make me happy. I might

have felt light physically but the emotional toll it took on me was heavy. And the pressure was going to increase as I was moving to Mumbai where I would have to see my husband surrounded by women who were way more petite and prettier than me. I was being immature but that's how I was feeling.

In Mumbai, my insecurity coupled with a sense of loss of identity led to sadness. I found a job, but my work wasn't giving me any satisfaction. I felt lost. I was always on one crazy diet and fitness regime or another. Soon I developed IBS – irritable bowel syndrome. I went to many doctors and all of them said my health problem stemmed from anxiety or an underlying emotional issue. Was I going through something?

Of course I was, but I didn't want to acknowledge it as I associated depression with weakness. So I buried my head like an ostrich, and hid my sickness from myself. Soon I started getting anxiety attacks. By this time I had two gorgeous kids, and my boy remained a loving partner, but my heart didn't have enough gratitude.

I pushed myself during the day, as I wanted to be the perfect mother, professional and wife, only to sink at night. My IBS became ten times worse. I felt bloated, got stomach cramps and sat in the bathroom for hours, pressing and squeezing my tummy, and I went through all this while being pregnant, twice. I could deal with the physical pain but not with the feeling of hopelessness.

My obsession with weight and size wasn't over yet. I started another weird diet where I ate baked namkeen and drank zero-calorie lemon-flavoured carbonated drinks the entire day. Then there was the time I gave up wheat and rice and ate only watermelon and peanuts.

I ended up sadder than before and my IBS was out of control. I still didn't link my depression to my physical issues and refused to see how they were connected. It was much easier to compartmentalize the IBS and tell myself I had a health issue that needed fixing.

I reached a point where I was crying five to six hours a night. Hopelessness and sadness were getting the better of me. That's when I learnt of Nichiren Buddhism and started chanting. It changed my life.

I started chanting because I was so affected by my professional life and unaccomplished goals that I linked them with my late-night tears and anxiety attacks. But chanting had an effect on every aspect of my life. I started experiencing happiness and personal victories on a completely new level.

My relationships, my temperament, everything improved in the most organic manner. It was as if the DNA of my being was transforming. The big stuff still needed fixing, but I came to realize that the way you look at something can stop it from becoming a problem.

I was slowly moving towards a happier me. But I still needed to work on my gut. That's when I went to an amazing Austrian health resort called VIVAMAYR. The resort was beautiful, nestled between a lake and mountains. The minute I stepped out of the car with my bags, I was dazzled by the beauty, my heart felt full and, above all, my lungs, clouded by an AQI of 300, felt cleansed.

VIVAMAYR's mission is detoxification – a complete cleansing of unhealthy toxins from the body. I started feeling these effects as soon as I checked in. Located away from the main city, it was totally quiet. The people there welcomed me with big smiles and in traditional clothes. This is what heaven must be like, I thought to myself.

But these angelic smiles started looking devilish two days into the detox. They just didn't give me enough food, no matter how much I pleaded or even tried to bribe them!

Everywhere I went things looked pristine and calm and gorgeous.

The reception and library area had jugs of water and herbal infusions in every nook and cranny. Anything to munch on? Oh no. The dining area had fixed seating where each individual was presented with medicines, oils and food strictly according to the diet prescribed for them.

Any chance of breaking the rules? No, it was worse than a boarding school. There was an outdoor area where I could snack on dollops of air after the measly meal. I sound deprived. Yes, I was. Little did I know things were about to get a whole lot worse.

'So . . .' That's how the staff began their sentences. Their English wasn't great but you could communicate with them provided your sentence began with 'so'. So my day started with visiting my doctor, an extremely hot guy who didn't mince words about my condition. He said that I was depressed.

His voice was soft and caressing, as if he was whispering sweet nothings in my ear, but his words were the opposite of orgasmic. That's the first time I acknowledged my condition. 'Yes, I know, but I am working to fix it. I have started chanting and—'

My hot doctor had already moved on to testing me for food intolerance. He asked me to lie down and held my hand, which I was most happy about. He made me hold a jar with a tiny bit of food in it and asked me to kick my raised leg. This is called kinesiology. Each time he said 'push' in his German accent, I felt like pulling him towards me. Unfortunately, I don't think he felt the same way. In fact, he looked more and more shocked each time he asked me to push.

It turned out that I was intolerant to – hold your breath – gluten (wheat, bread, etc.), lentils (all sorts of dals), eggs, all fruits, all nuts and lactose. To top it all I am a vegetarian! 'That covers practically everything!' I wailed. He tried to sound hopeful but even he couldn't manage it when he said I could eat gluten-free flour and vegetables.

By now my Buddha life state had gone for a toss. I called up the one person I could rant to. 'Should I buy a f**king oxygen cylinder to live? They have taken everything off my diet.' And before he could say anything I banged the phone down.

My love for food has been eternal. From stealing my juniors' tiffin boxes and taking up home science as an elective subject in tenth grade because it meant

I could bake cakes, cook and eat in class to joining the athletic team as they were the only kids who got a banana shake and sandwiches after practice, food has driven my life (something I deprived myself of later, which perhaps was a trigger for my depression), so much so that my boy even had to bring brownies to our dates to score some brownie points before we made out. Want more proof? My two short films are called *Toffee* and *Pinni*.

And then it hit me. At least someone was pointing to a definite cause for my pain, instead of leaving me at 'are you stressed' and then putting me on antacids for months. I decided to take up this next challenge joyfully and let go of everything I was intolerant to. Chanting had given me the wisdom to approach this moment with grace.

I returned to India a new person. I felt amazing, and for the first time in ten years I didn't have stomach cramps or bloating. There was another silver lining. The doctors at VIVAMAYR said that since I was not allergic but only intolerant to these foods, I'd be able to return to eating them in time, once my gut recovered. I was extremely happy and ready to be healed, only to be diagnosed with breast cancer within a month.

9

No matter how many voices at
you do scream
Don't let that stop you from following your
dream

I was one of those people who really didn't know what career they wanted to pursue. I had a long list of 'maybe this is what I want to do' which I was happy to tick off. I see many people like me who try to figure out their options by the process of elimination. But if I am honest, I think I always knew what I wanted to be; I was just too scared to dream.

This lack of confidence and vision was accompanied by my wish to be with my boy. So he continued doing what he wanted to do, and that's how it should be, but I made my life choices adjusting to his world. This had to get to me one day, and it did. More on this later.

Financial stability was of utmost importance to my middle-class family. I had to have a job, no matter what, and so I started working when I was still in college. At university I picked up part-time jobs and earned enough to spend on my dates and sustain myself. I never had to ask my parents for money and have been working ever since.

However, there was another side to my personality that gave me tremendous happiness and satisfaction. Theatre. Through college, I took part in all the youth festival plays. There weren't any independent theatre groups at the time so all of us enthusiasts in the college theatre circuit formed our own independent group.

We called ourselves Manch Tantra and declared it a professional theatre group.

We wanted to break the image of theatre being associated with strugglers – the chai and sutta variety – and create a company that could potentially be a source of income. Our first production, conceptualized by me, was called *Socha Na Tha*. We managed to book the Tagore Theatre, a famous auditorium in Chandigarh. The day arrived. Curtains went up, the house was packed, the press was present, we performed.

The next day, the press ripped us apart. But that didn't discourage us. We just started calling ourselves an amateur theatre group instead. We staged many productions thereafter and they did well. But as college ended, and our batch spread out looking for jobs, we shut shop.

A few of us left for Mumbai, some joined the corporate sector, others joined the army. I remained confused. While my heart was in theatre and writing, I saw them only as hobbies.

And yet I remained driven, so driven that on the last day of university, instead of celebrating with friends, I drove to my office. One of my part-time jobs at college was at Shaan PR, a public relations agency run by Aneesh and Shanti Bhanot, a wonderful couple who taught me a lot about work and ethics, and life. I was good at the job and decided it was what I wanted to do once I finished my master's. So I opened up my own PR company called Direct Relations.

My office was a single room, generously given to me by family friends Kiran aunty and Tonto uncle. They had a floor for their businesses and this small room was vacant, and I will always be grateful to them for giving it to me.

So this fresh postgraduate's business card read CEO, for which I was mocked a lot. But I did some good work. From being the office boy, the executive making calls, writing up the press releases, talking to clients, carrying standees along with the press kits for events and, yes, to also being the CEO, I was a one-woman army. My reputation picked up and I got decent clients.

But my heart wasn't in it. Two years on, I diversified into event management and held a successful exhibition with around sixty exhibitors at Hotel Shivalikview, Chandigarh. But overconfidence and lack of wisdom killed the business. An exhibition at Ludhiana was a huge failure, so much so that I had to stand at the gates and demand clients for the money they owed me. A male client rudely shoved me out of the way. It was a nightmare and I was only twenty-four.

This setback along with my lack of enthusiasm for the work led to the closure of Direct Relations. I joined BIG 92.7 FM as the programming head in Jalandhar, where my nani lived. My game plan was to work so hard that they would transfer me to Mumbai, where my boy was working for MTV.

You might ask what is so wrong with putting someone you love before you. The mistake was not loving myself enough, and not figuring out things for myself, which I would regret later. But I want to say here that my boy never pressurized me to make these decisions. He would have supported me no matter what I chose.

I got engaged and was doing well at the radio station. I was even named the best programming head of the north division. No sooner did I get the award than I put in my papers. Like in every other job, I wasn't excited any more. Besides, the wedding was in three months and my only focus was on preparing for the D-Day and then moving to Mumbai.

For the next few months, all my energy was directed towards – and I am not proud of this – losing weight. I lost ten kilos along with a lot of brain cells. Happily married, I reached Mumbai with the sole mission of staying thin.

What the f**k was I even thinking? To the world my life may not appear to have had any real challenges, but most of our struggles are the battles we fight within. These internal, invisible problems are equally, if not more, difficult to overcome than the more evident, real-world ones. I had started to feel empty.

I wrote only to kill time, not realizing that I was choosing writing over other things I could do to kill time. I couldn't see where my happiness lay. I had passed the UGC NET exam during my university days, which made me eligible for lectureship anywhere in the country. So I started teaching mass communication and journalism classes at various colleges in Mumbai and pretty much had my Sushmita Sen moment from *Main Hoon Na*.

Of course, I wasn't teaching in chiffon saris. I wore trousers and shirts. I enjoyed lecturing and had almost 100 per cent attendance on most days. Many of my fellow teachers attributed my success to my clothing, so the college announced that female lecturers could only wear kurtas. I started teaming my jeans with knee-length kurtas. My attendance was the same. This was followed by another announcement asking us to wear dupattas.

In the meantime, I became a Reebok-certified aerobics trainer and started teaching in my society, which became another source of income for me. I was getting annoyed with the petty college politics. I liked the teaching part of the job but not much else. And by liked I mean I liked it well enough. It didn't make me want to jump in front of a Mumbai local train and kill myself. It was a respectable, secure job and I held on to it. Then one day I did the inevitable.

By now my sadness was really creeping up on me.

I considered myself a stupid, uncommitted person who was only good at putting in resignation papers. My personal life gave me happiness, but I cannot say the same about my professional life.

I continued writing, and it kept me afloat. I wrote three books. The first was a novel, the second a collection of short stories and for the third, a publisher approached me. I said to myself, 'Wow, yes, I have made it!' Then he said, 'Madam, you have to write about your husband and his journey to Bollywood. You can be the co-author.'

No points for guessing which of the three grabbed maximum eyeballs, bringing me back to the questions: Who am I? What do I want? What is my identity? The consequences of not respecting yourself creep up on you eventually.

I truly believed my kid was more sorted than me. Milk time, sleep time, massage time, colic time. And repeat, milk time, sleep time . . . look at the focus! And here I was all over the place, but actually nowhere.

Mumbai became daunting, so on the pretext that my husband was too busy for my son and me I would go running back to Chandigarh and spend months with my parents. I was being an escapist. The next time I went to Mumbai to meet my husband I ended up getting pregnant again!

Thanks to some really excited Punjabi hormones (of which you are already aware), before I knew it I was pregnant for the second time and back in Chandigarh. I told myself, 'Enough!' Yes, enough of getting pregnant but, more importantly, enough of sinking!

So I resurrected our theatre group in Chandigarh, which hadn't done a production in eleven years, with my friend Aviral, another ex-member of Manch Tantra. With my tummy getting bigger and bigger, we put out a play based on my second book, *Souled Out*.

The play, which I directed, was received very well. We had to stage two shows in Chandigarh in the infamous Tagore Theatre and another two in Delhi. It was redemption for me, getting love and appreciation on the stage where I had been ridiculed, eleven years on.

The experience was wonderful but the feeling didn't last long, as everyone around the project moved on with their lives, leaving me yet again in limbo. I now had two beautiful babies and a wonderful happy husband, but the sinking feeling was stronger than ever.

I started writing again. I wrote scripts, short films, screenplays. I took them to a couple of people, only to be rejected. I took these rejections too seriously, and for the next five years I kept writing with no hope of anyone reading, let alone appreciating, my work.

My life was a mess, but it was a mess only to me. To everyone else I had two kids, a happy home, a husband who was doing well – what was the problem? The only thing that gave me happiness was writing and being involved with theatre and arts in some way.

But bringing up two kids, I didn't allow myself to dream. My boy was mostly travelling for shoots and concerts, but whatever time he spent in Mumbai he was there for us. I can't blame him. I can't blame anyone but myself as I never made an attempt to put myself first. As mentioned earlier, I had now spiralled into an ugly phase where I would cry for five to six hours every night. In the morning I would pretend to be happy and cheerful as I couldn't afford to look like a loser in front of my kids.

I didn't seek any medical help despite having anxiety attacks almost every day. When the attacks got really bad, I would lie down and press my chest against the pillow to try and stop my heart from beating so fast. I thought it would explode.

The new normal of being depressed and leading a double life of being happy in the day and the exact opposite at night was eating into me.

And then one day, the universe gave me a second chance. My friend Sukriti came home for a playdate along with another friend, Henna. As luck would have it, they had been practising a lovely philosophy called Nichiren Buddhism. Sukriti had, in fact, tried to introduce me to it ten years ago while we were still in college.

Back then I had laughed at her. Today I was the one seeking help. To be honest, I took up the practice out of desperation and not from a place of faith. I wanted to do one right thing before the situation became worse. I was too afraid to see what it would be like if I degenerated further.

The beautiful part is that the practice itself says, 'Test me.' And I gave it my all, whatever little was left of me. As I wrote in the previous chapter, the chanting changed the very DNA of my being. It changed my thinking and my attitude, and when these changed, the world around me also started to look better. I truly started believing that it wasn't too late for me. And I finally admitted to myself that I wanted to focus on my writing and take my love for theatre to the next level and become a film-maker.

I gave up all my fears. If I made a bad film, people might think, 'Actor ki biwi hai, velli hai, thoda time pass kar rahi hai.' My ex-students might ridicule me and say, 'Humein kya padha rahi thi, we can do better than this.' Worst of all, what if the film didn't see the light of day or was ripped apart like my first play? I was nineteen then. At thirty-four I had much more at stake. What if I brought shame to my husband who had already made a name for himself?

Chanting gave me the courage and wisdom to dream. Not just have dreams but to have goals and the intention to accomplish them.

'We have the power to change our destiny.' 'The reason we are born is not to suffer but to strive to be happy.' 'The universe is like your own personal bank account, the amount of fortune you can withdraw depends on your faith, and faith means fighting life's negative tendencies.' I started living by these powerful guidelines.

My driving point, my passion, my calling had always been there in front of me, but my path was clouded because I lacked faith in myself. It took me twelve years to acknowledge my dreams and begin to try and fulfil them.

To some my struggle might not be struggle enough as it didn't involve sleeping on a railway platform or living off Tiger biscuits. But, as I said before, some struggles are internal and they are just as difficult to overcome.

Soon after, I made my first short film, *Toffee*. It was nominated for the best short film and got screened at many prestigious film festivals, including the Taiwan International Children's Film Festival. It was the only Indian entry to be screened, and that too alongside a Cannes award winner.

When we were invited for the festival, my husband and I decided to attend. It was the first time someone was paying for my travel and stay. Of course, my boy had to pay for his. Once we reached Taipei, he got out of the airport first and was looking for someone holding a placard with his name.

I was doing the same. As I scanned the crowds, my boy came running and pulled me by my arm to a corner, where I saw a man wearing a black suit and black sunglasses holding a placard. It said 'Tahira Kashyap'. There, my identity.

It was a proud moment for me, especially when

I saw the pride in my partner's eyes. My boy had always supported me, but that day I realized he also had dreams for me.

The only thing that bothered me was that my boy was one of the producers of the film. It might not matter to some but it did to me. My worries were put to rest when Eros Now came on board and officially bought the film from the producers, and today they are presenting it.

I recently made another short film called *Pinni*, which received a lot of love, but as I write this book I still haven't made my feature film. But this time I have no intention of giving up. This is my calling, and I am ready to wait for my chance for the rest of my life.

10

Be atmanirbhar
Say no to Chinese food, even ghar par

The first time you have an unplanned baby you can call it carelessness and maybe bad (or good) luck. Now to have two unplanned babies in this modern era of contraception is not carelessness – it's called being Punjabi.

Let me take you back to the night I became a rodeo rider. Our son was one and a half years old and any parent who has lived through this phase will understand when I say that motherhood might be bliss on occasion, but it also makes you want to break free. I have to be honest, there were many, many moments when I doubted if this was what I wanted!

I was either feeding, burping, massaging or walking him. I would work out with him crawling around, and as a first-time parent I was so paranoid that I kept his bassinet by the bathroom door while I tried to finish my routine in exactly fifteen minutes.

One minute more and the colicky baby would start crying.

Even the once-in-a-while sex was interrupted by his sadistic wails. I would drop everything and rush to him feeling guilty. Do I sound heartless? Mothers who have just delivered a baby must be nodding as they read this; I don't need to explain myself.

All new parents know how much planning goes into deciding the one night you want some action. Spontaneity toh bhul jao! Sex takes days and days of working around the little monster's routine. Moreover, you have to train yourself to feel horny in the exact two hours between his feeds, which is no small feat.

Once in a while the stars align. Feeding, check; burping, check; baby asleep, yes! Everything is going smoothly for once. You slip into the lingerie that you haven't used since leap year (it's nine months for the normal world, but ask a pregnant lady, the gestation period feels endless, as if you are waiting for the next 29 February). The boy is also showing off his nicely trimmed chest hair.

The mood is right; yes, tonight we are going to score. And right at that moment the baby decides to wail his small lungs out because, nope, it's not the poop, it's not the feed, it's . . . just because. That's it. No reason. Timepass. Practising his vocals so he can perhaps jam with his father on 'Paani da rang' some day.

This is how I arrived at my theory of babies being sadists. I told you I wouldn't justify myself, but I did. Why? Ufff, yeh guilt. The feeling that has been there with me from girlhood through womanhood and now motherhood. Has someone made me feel guilty? Is there anyone to blame? No. Is it conditioning? Can it be worked on? Yes.

Let me return to the main story – the night I became a rodeo rider. My parents were visiting us. After you have a kid, you love your parents just a little bit more. Of course, you appreciate all that they have done for you in a new way, but they are also the only people you can surrender the baby to guilt-free. No baby latching on to me. Yes, yes, yes! I could finally get my upper lip threaded. What a bonus!

In gratitude I got Chinese food made at home that night. It's my parents' favourite cuisine. Then came the moment, the one we had both been waiting for. 'Say it, say it,' my boy's and my thought bubbles were screaming. As if hearing our innermost wishes, my mother said, 'Let Virajveer sleep with us while we are here.'

'Yessssss!' Our thought bubbles were making out already. So after a hearty meal of chowmein, my husband and I retreated to our room. I completely agree with the idiot who said 'Chow mein kha kar dimaag garam ho jaata hai.' We were proving his idiotic theory right. Next thing I know I had become a full-fledged rodeo rider.

We had the most amazing sex, but later realized that the ajinomoto in the noodles had blinded us and we hadn't used protection. I was about to pop the twenty-four-hour contraceptive pill, but I started menstruating that night, in fact, that very moment. It wasn't the chowmein but the high levels of estrogen that had taken me so spectacularly down the home stretch.

Since I got my periods, I thought there was no need to take the pill. Here I was, a goddamn science student, and I had messed up basic biology. I had forgotten that it takes just one sperm to fertilize a woman's egg.

To meet the lonely little waiting egg, the mighty semen must travel from the vagina to the fallopian tubes, a journey equivalent to a Roadies task that only few can survive. Par mera pati toh Roadie tha, toh uska sperm bhi Roadie hoga!

Despite all the above-mentioned odds, that one tiny sperm rock-climbed its way to prove that unplanned babies can happen twice over.

Now, of course, we didn't know what the clever sperm was up to or for how many days it was hiding in my uterus. So things went back to normal, with the memory of our rodeo night beautifully etched in our minds.

A few weeks later, Simran, my favourite cousin, called me from Pune to tell me his wife was pregnant. I was really happy for them.

As soon as I kept the phone down, I realized I had skipped my periods. I galloped to the chemist and bought ten pregnancy kits, all different brands. One had Neha Marda on it, my husband's first co-star in a TV series. It was a weird feeling. I took the tests. And for the first time in my life I got a perfect ten on ten.

How could this have possibly happened? Seeing our stubborn, feisty little girl now, I can imagine how resilient she would have been even as a four-cell embryo. And so the next call was from me to Simran in Pune. They laughed and laughed, of course, at my expense. History was going to repeat itself. Simran and I shared a birthday. Our daughters, too, would be born around the same time.

The husband was equally shocked when he came home. He saw how disturbed I was and suggested we go out for dinner. I agreed. He said, 'A very good Chinese restaurant has opened nearby.' I swear, I felt like strangling him there and then with a noodle or two.

11

**Don't expect to be like Raj and Simran
in marriage
You're more likely to be riding a
one-wheel carriage**

My life has always been in sync with the Bollywood life my boy lives on-screen. In his first movie he was a generous sperm donor. The donations had already happened on the home front. While he was shooting, I was expanding, and when the movie finally came out, I, too, popped out the first baby.

In those days I was extremely foolish and insecure. My boy was also too immature to sit me down and help me understand things, and we did not have any family or close friends in the film industry to explain its workings. No one in my family could relate to my issues, so I had to struggle through them alone. After all, no one had seen their husbands kiss or woo other girls on-screen. I had a major problem with all this.

The divide between my boy and me was increasing by the day. I remember one time when my husband was nominated for the best debut actor. Both of us looked our best and were extremely excited about the night. He was used to the glitz and the madness, having hosted many award shows before he made his acting debut, but it was a first for me.

I did not anticipate the hysteria around such a night. As soon as we reached the venue, I saw blinding flashlights that completely dazed me. My boy and I walked down the red carpet hand in hand. I was all nerves and overwhelmed by the hundreds of eyes fixed on us.

To begin with, I was trying to remember the name of the designer whose gown I was wearing. I hadn't heard the name before and was told the press might ask what I was wearing on the red carpet. So I kept rehearsing the goddamn tongue-twister of a name, only to discover later that everybody knew him.

So there I was, walking the red carpet, conscious about how I was looking, trying to remember the designer's name, blinded by the lights. And suddenly I couldn't feel the warmth of his hand. It had been the only comforting thing in that ordeal, and I no longer had it. He had left me behind and was up ahead, surrounded by the press.

I froze, not knowing where to go, fighting my tears. I didn't want to create a scene, but I guess I already was a scene, standing there like a dimwit. After a few minutes I saw him coming back for me, looking worried.

Of course, he apologized profusely; it had been a simple mistake. Today I can see it from his point of view, but back then I held it against him for the longest time. Because of this stupid incident we couldn't enjoy the moment he was awarded best debutant that year.

There were many such episodes, and we only survived them because of how long we had been together. The foundation of our relationship was rock solid. Amid all the chaos I knew he wasn't a bad boy, and amid all the confusion I was creating for him he knew I wasn't a malicious person. And so we moved on.

But all my fears came back with his next film, *Nautanki Saala!*, where sir participated in one of the longest kisses in the history of Indian cinema, at least that's what the articles said. I was burning with jealousy. My anger and insecurity crossed Virat Kohli's runs.

I never went to my boy's sets. He was too

conscious; that's how he has always been. I knew this but my insecurities were getting the better of me, and I blamed him for hiding things from me. So one day, to put my fears to rest, he invited me to come with him.

Sets are boring when you have nothing to contribute to the process of film-making. After seeing him sway his pelvis for forty-five minutes for one song sequence, I lost my patience and really didn't care if he made out after. I had had enough of the boring shoot and left the venue.

My boy kept trying to soothe my fears as best he could and asked me to come with him on his promotional tour. As I was driving with him and the director in the car, the latter was talking about how people were loving the kissing scene, how it was hilarious, kiss . . . something . . . kiss . . . something something . . . kiss . . . kiss. All I heard was the one word I didn't want to.

I saw that my boy was feeling uncomfortable. I could also sense that his discomfort was not about the kiss itself but for me having to hear of it. Our past, as I said, helped us sail through these tricky moments, but we never really resolved our issues.

His next film was *Dum Laga Ke Haisha*. A small-town flashback: once at university some of us girls were soaking in the winter sun and chatting on the lush green lawns in between lectures.

We played a game about who would get married first, and then came to the big question – what did we want our first night to be like?

Now this is the influence of films on our lives. At least five out of the eight girls dreamt of their husbands sweeping them off their feet and carrying them in their strong, muscular arms to bed.

I glanced at my skinny boy who was throwing peanuts in the air and catching them in his mouth. At that time there was a difference of exactly ten kilos in our weights – I was sixty-eight kilos and he weighed fifty-eight.

So when it was my turn to reveal my deepest desires, I started with us walking towards the bed. I think the girls all knew how unlikely their fantasy would be for me.

After all those years, that winter day's conversation still lingered in my head. Since I had lost weight, one day after the wedding I asked him to carry me to the bed to prove a point. I was a dainty girl now and was ready to be swept off my feet. This was way out of character for me, something my boy hadn't signed up for.

He asked if something was wrong with me. But I didn't want to hear another word and insisted that he pick me up and take me to the bed. The mood had changed between us from playfulness to disbelief to irritation. Eventually, with much reluctance, he did fulfil my request.

I would be lying if I say his arms didn't shake, but somehow I reached the bed. I tried to stay as still as possible and to make it as easy for him as I could, but the whole exercise was pointless and uncomfortable. By the time we got to the bed, both of us were sweating and the mood was tense. Needless to say, this grand gesture did not result in any consequential act. But at least we got a good workout.

So when *Dum Laga Ke Haisha* happened, I was annoyed. Here he was, willingly carrying a girl who weighed twenty kilos more than him. I would say passive-aggressive things like, 'Where there is a will there is a way. You never wanted to pick me up, I guess. How could you pick her up so easily?' He would get frustrated and reply that he had been practising for months. He had to carry his gym trainer on his back to prepare for the film.

I wanted to yell back that if he had practised with me all these years, he wouldn't have needed his trainer. Instead, I sulked. I told him it was clear that for films he 'happily' did the very things which seemed like forced errands to him at home.

He lost his patience and said, 'What do you want?' I didn't know what I wanted, as being picked up and taken to the bed had never been on my agenda. But by then we were too deep into our fight and I needed to save face. So I said, 'I want to be picked up, too.' He threw his hands up in the air and said, 'Fine'.

I was ready to be carried like a baby, but instead he picked me up and tossed me on his back like a gunny bag and stomped around the house, as if we were at a sabzi mandi. 'What the hell are you doing?' I asked. He put me down and said, 'This is the only way I have trained.' I rolled my eyes and kept quiet. So, you see, I still hadn't made friends with his career.

Thankfully, in the middle of this crazy, unreasonable behaviour came Buddhism. I have described it as the great saviour in life because that's how it felt for me.

When I started chanting, all the knots in my head which had filled my brain like tangled balls of wool began to slowly unravel. Chanting touched on every problem I was facing – depression, weight, health, jealousy; they were all connected and self-created. It changed my outlook, generated feelings of positivity and helped me become aware of the issues I was facing, giving me the strength and wisdom to deal with them. I didn't even notice these changes in myself.

A few years later, I was sitting with my boy in Sriram Raghavan's office and we were watching the edit of *Andhadhun*. I thoroughly enjoyed the movie. As I stepped out, the team asked me for my feedback. One of the points I made really surprised my boy.

I said, 'Their (Radhika Apte and my boy's) make-out scene ends abruptly. I think we are jumping to the next scene too quickly. I want to be with the characters a little longer.'

To my surprise the feedback – I am sure others would have made the same point – was taken, and in the final version of the film we see Radhika making a messy breakfast of eggs the next morning.

Did you notice the change, too? It happened so organically that I didn't see it. But my boy did. From someone who threw tantrums over his love scenes to now giving him suggestions on making out with the actress, I truly had come a long way.

I had finally understood that acting is an art. The actor has to stay true to the character, the plot and the vision of the director. Of course, I had known all this, but somehow I hadn't really absorbed it. Recognizing it completely liberated me. And to give my boy his due, he has given me enough reasons to be secure, not just by words, in fact, never by his words.

I learnt my lesson too well and took the empathy for my husband's craft to the next level. When he had to play a bald guy in his next film, *Bala*, I gave him company off-screen by going bald. Of course, that was a result of my chemotherapy, but I like to believe, as I said earlier, that my life has pretty much been in sync with the Bollywood life my boy lives on-screen. Oh, by the way, I just found out that his next film is about a man who stabs his wife ... gulp.

12

**Don't worry about being a perfect mommy
The kids still manage to grow up nicely**

The first book I wrote was called *I Promise*. It was based on my play *Socha Na Tha*. The protagonist was a pyre maker and a perfectionist. For him burning pyres was an art and he did it with dedication and precision.

I didn't realize I was writing about myself when I wrote that character, not the pyre-making part, but being a perfectionist. This obsessive-compulsive part of me also meant I was always tying myself up in knots.

In school I wore my hair in a braid held up by four bobby pins, two on each side. The clips looked identical but I knew which side I wore them on and they couldn't swap places, so I placed them exactly like that on the dressing table after removing them, the left ones on the left side and the right ones on the right. It used to make my blood boil if Mama mixed them up.

As I grew up I picked up more idiosyncrasies, such as parking the car with the tyres aligned and always leaving it in second gear, arranging my pillow a certain way before sleeping and wearing only certain shades of underwear. So, yeah, I was crazy. And we all know what motherhood can do to you. If you aren't crazy already, it makes you so. And if you were crazy before (like me), it makes you crazier.

So once these two small beings entered my life, I began to take the role of a mother way too seriously. I charted my days with the precision of a robot. No matter how much help I had at home, only I gave my kids their bath and dressed them up, fed them breakfast, combed their hair and then sent them to school.

Even if I had slept at 2 or 3 a.m., I was up every day at 6 a.m. to dress my children and send them off. I was so caught up in the small things – their nails being trimmed, their uniforms ironed, clean socks, bags, tiffins – that sometimes I missed the larger picture.

Once I dropped off my immaculately groomed kids to school on a public holiday. I had woken up that morning thinking of my to-do list, forgetting it wasn't a to-do kind of day, and powered through the morning with my usual efficiency. The kids really cursed me that day.

My brain was so flooded with these mundane things that there was no way it could have made space for any other information to creep in, no matter how consequential it was.

This is how my day looked. I'd be up at six to get my kids ready for school, then worked on my writing, had meetings, gave script narrations, travelled, did the occasional shoot, and also ran the home and the kids' routines. Since I also wanted to stay up to meet my boy, who more often than not would be back late at night because of his own shoots, I would end up sleeping at 2 or 3 a.m. Now I know most women would say, 'What's so heroic in it? We do it all the time.' And the men, too, seem to expect this 24/7 devotion to the home, the kids and themselves.

But, ladies, let me tell you. It may not be heroic, but it is insane and inhuman to sleep for only four hours when you can get more only if you put yourself at the centre of your universe. Sadly, it took cancer for me to understand that I needed to let some things go and realize that things can bloom on their own, without my divine intervention, and that I needed to bloom, too.

During my treatment, I was often not home and unable to do much. I ran around for my tests, spent eight days in hospital for my surgery and on returning home, remained quite weak for some time. The kids managed very well on their own, with help from my husband and parents. Of course, they couldn't match up to my idea of perfection, but they managed.

When my daughter came to my room after school, I saw that only eight of her fingernails were clipped. Our help had forgotten to clip the nails of the thumbs. I can't blame anyone as I had always clipped my kids' nails.

But did the sky collapse because the nails weren't trimmed? Did I get a stinker from the school? Did her friends stop talking to her? Did she fail at her recital? No, everything was just as before. And my reaction changed to laughing over her tiny untrimmed nails rather than fretting over them.

The menu for the tiffin boxes had changed, with a few new inclusions by my mother. On Thursdays the kids stopped getting their wholesome besan ka chila and took home-made French fries instead. Now for

Mama's generation this wasn't unhealthy but for us it was sacrilege. However, I learnt to let go.

Earlier, I would have freaked out at this unhealthy addition to their meals. But I told myself that this was once a week and helped the kids bond with their grandmother. And so instead of stressing I made sure they took along ketchup and a fruit.

Suddenly I had the headspace and energy to have meaningful conversations with my kids, ranging from what their favourite author Dr Seuss looked like and what he was thinking when he wrote his crazy books about the universe and its wonders. We talked about the many countries in the world and how different places were in different time zones.

Along with me, my kids, too, underwent a deep transformation, and the next time my five-year-old daughter made sure all her fingernails were clipped. I learnt to trust, and they learnt to be responsible.

We spoke about how people look different but feel the same emotions. I spoke at length about Buddhism and its principles to them, about the compassion, wisdom and courage that this philosophy preaches. We also spoke about my health and my battle with cancer. I heard stories about their friends and school and learnt about their take on relationships and happiness. I gave them something, and they gave me a whole lot back.

They aren't all little angels

Now before you think that my kids are wonderful, mature little angels, let me assure you that is not the case. Kids are unpredictable. If you want to show off to your friend that your baby has been toilet-trained, the baby will let out a huge gaseous cannonball along with a heap of poop right then. And if you boast to your pals about how your child has never snatched anything from other kids or cheated at school, the child will magically appear in the middle of your living room and do exactly the opposite, perhaps snatch the biscuit that was to go into your friend's mouth. Kids are very true to their character, let's give them that at least. They will never stop being unpredictable.

Now in the current situation of coronavirus and the lockdown, one would think there are hardly any opportunities available to kids to embarrass us. But then, again, we would be undermining their superhero abilities.

I was on a Zoom call with my friends. As we were expressing our desperation to meet each other, my little one pops her head into the frame and says, 'Mama, isn't that your friend whom you were saying you will never meet as she isn't following the rules and doesn't stay home during the lockdown?' Of course, at such moments when you want your technology to throw up a glitch, the reception was crystal clear. I shoved her aside, trying to laugh off my silly daughter and her nonsense chatter, but the damage was done, and my friend hasn't come for any Zoom call thereafter. There are plenty of such embarrassing incidents that have cost me not just friendships but jobs, too!

Earlier this year, my boy was in a film called *Shubh Mangal Saavdhaan*, the story of two gay men in love with each other. We haven't yet taken our kids to see his films as they are too young to separate the character on-screen from their father – if you recall, I had the same problem for a while.

We did try once with another of his films. On that occasion, I convinced my boy that we should take our kids to the cinema hall the way our parents took us. And so we stepped into the theatre discreetly, my boy with his hoodie on, after the movie started.

I was really happy, savouring the moment and also my mixed popcorn. And then all hell broke loose. Both the kids started howling – not sobbing or crying but wailing their lungs out – when they saw their father being humiliated in one scene. The hoodie that my boy wore was used to wipe their tears and running noses. So much for being discreet.

We promised each other that we weren't going to repeat this ever again. And that was the last of it, but with the movie on gay love releasing soon, I knew my eight-year-old son's friends would perhaps hear about it and mention it or tease him.

So I mustered all my courage to address the issue. I sat down my son and asked him, 'Do you know what being gay is?' To my surprise he said yes. I probed him further and he said, 'When a boy likes a boy, that's being gay.'

I could sense that he was saying this without

understanding the sexual implication. Cautiously, I asked him if he was okay with it. He said, 'What is there not to be okay with? A boy and a girl can like each other. Similarly, a boy and a boy can also like each other. That is what compassion means.' And with that he got up from the table and went back to playing with his Lego.

I was gobsmacked. It was that easy for him. He may not have grasped the sexual aspect of it, but he had understood that we need to be tolerant of each other, even if we are different. Gay or not, how can we judge?

If it's so easy for an eight-year-old to accept this, I fail to understand what is taking the world so long. I wondered if my little boy had understood this idea because of our conversations about compassion. It's hard to know exactly what gave him this wisdom and clarity.

But it was the most gratifying experience to discover that I had created this kid who could think so clearly, so sensitively. This was the kid I had to bring with me to the bathroom when he was an infant because I was so paranoid. The kid who I bathed and fed and over whose lunch box I slaved. Somewhere in the middle of all that anxious overparenting, he had slipped from my controlling grasp and become a person all by himself. What was the point of obsessing and micromanaging?

That day I was truly proud of my parenting, or should I say un-parenting. Oh no, did I just say proud ... waiting for the unpredictable species to attack!

13

Stressed your cup is half-empty, not full?
Remember you need to always stay grateful

I am thirty-five and my boy and I are on the roads of Delhi. We are here because of my increased breast size. For someone who had to stuff handkerchiefs in her training bra in school, this sudden, belated growth of my breast was a quantum leap.

This called for a celebration, but it was a partial celebration as the growth was only on one side. The dimwit that I was, I thought the other side would soon catch up. Soon there was a secretion from the heavier breast. Several tests took me from having under a 2 per cent chance of contracting breast cancer to 30 per cent after a mammogram to 70 per cent after an MRI and finally 95 per cent after the biopsy. A mammoth promotion!

If the microbes in my microbiology class in college had grown at this speed, instead of at the rate of the hair growth of someone who was taking homoeopathic hairfall treatment, my biotechnology classes would have been less torturous. Additionally, this kind of jump in the budget of my film would have allowed me to travel with my pillow in first class.

So this is why my boy and I were in Delhi – to get an MRI-led biopsy which was only available there. We went directly to the hospital after a two-hour flight where we spent the time playing noughts and crosses. Thankfully, our eight-year-old son, who never loses a game, wasn't with us and so we were giving tough competition to each other.

We walked down the corridors of the hospital in a daze, trying to find the right room. We had accumulated, on the way, a bevy of onlookers who were following us from floor to floor courtesy of my actor husband.

The doctor stapled my breast to get a sample for the biopsy and even before the results arrived, she knew it was some stage of cancer. She took us to her room and showed us the various stages of cancer on her laptop. Both of us were dumbstruck. One is never ready for such things. And at that moment we didn't fully absorb it.

A couple of giggling nurses interrupted us as we sat there numb. The doctor sighed, looked at my husband and said, 'Can they please have a selfie with you? They are huge fans.'

The poor husband didn't know how to react as only a few minutes ago he had learnt that his wife had cancer. He grinned like a zombie. The nurses had the audacity to say, 'Sir, you are not looking good in this one, let's take another.' 'For f**k's sake,' I thought to myself.

During our thirty-minute ride to the hotel, we were completely quiet, unable to say a word to each other. When we got to our room, I finally broke the silence. I looked at him and said, 'Bh*****d, lag gayi.'

Both of us burst out laughing. Something changed in that moment. From shock and fear we moved to positivity and determination. I looked at my boy – my boyfriend of seventeen years and husband of nine. We were in this together, we were going to cross this hurdle.

My doctor in Mumbai, Dr Mandar, gave me the good news and the bad. The former was that I was stage 0 breast cancer, a case of early detection and conducive to treatment and cure. The latter was that I needed a mastectomy because the cancer had spread across the whole breast.

Yikes, losing something that had meant my entire life to me! I was devastated. My boy saw my face fall and said I was insane to obsess about my breasts over my life. And, of course, he was right.

The doctor also suggested we get the reconstruction done during the same surgery. I gathered my wits and said that he should seize this opportunity and stuff the biggest cups he could – D, E, F – in there. He ignored my comment, using the tissues from my back to reconstruct the breast and matching its size to my other humble one.

I still tell the doctors that we lost a golden opportunity – finally I could have risen to the ranks of Kim and Pam. I thought of my new breast as the nouveau riche one, since it was a size bigger owing to post-op swelling. Sadly, it began to deflate no sooner than I started to like it. Today I am exactly where my journey had begun.

My learnings and observations. Many people associate diseases with pent-up emotions, negativity, dark secrets and bad food habits, and if I show any sign of agreement, my doctors will kill me as there isn't any research that proves this. But I do believe that the intention of self-destruction can actually lead you there.

I had many things that went against me in life and far more things that worked in my favour. Previously, I had chosen to see the negative and now, because of the chanting, I was beginning to love myself. I have never felt happier with myself than right now. And it's an amazing feeling.

My diet has improved, my intentions have improved, my thoughts and actions are focused on preserving and conserving myself. But I still have to work on my obsession with getting a D cup. It's a work in progress, but I am getting there! Jokes apart, negative thoughts do express themselves as do positive affirmations.

When I was diagnosed with cancer, all I knew was that I was ready to cope with it. My practice tells me that the only reason we are faced with an obstacle is for us to become a better version of ourselves. It is an opportunity to change something in our life and a springboard to achieve greater heights.

I chanted through my ordeal and was supported by the prayers of many people, known and unknown. That's the beauty of this practice where we not only chant for our own happiness but also for others.

Despite the surgery and the chemotherapy and its side effects, my life force was strong and I went to work every single day, with the exception of weekends when my chemotherapy sessions were scheduled.

I shed my hair, along with all the inhibitions and complexes I had accumulated over so many years. I no longer aimed to hit the fifties on the weighing scale. I loved my body and my bald head. I didn't feel envious or insecure any more and only had love to share.

After the surgery, Dr Mandar asked me, 'How's your wound? Is there too much pain? How are you feeling? Any complaints?' I nodded and said, 'Yes, I do have a complaint. Doc, I am ... uhh ... I am constipated.' He looked at me in disbelief and walked away without saying a word.

He came back the next day and I still had the same issue. He got cross and said, 'You had surgery. A major one. Just reminding you. Any problem associated with that?' I sheepishly shook my head.

As the doctor left, I realized the meaning of his words. I had just undergone a major surgery. Why was I not feeling the trauma and pain associated with it? It was because of my determination and the faith of my comrades that I could go through this phase joyously. Though I wished I had prayed for relief from my constipation, too!

But on a serious note, there wasn't a single day when I said 'Why me?' Of course, I have my moments. Each time I head for a blood test or scan I am anxious, but chanting helps me maintain my sanity and have deep gratitude.

So I had my mastectomy and reconstruction in an eight-hour surgery. I had twelve chemotherapy sessions, over twelve weeks. The last two were the toughest. The medicine in your bloodstream doesn't just wash away; it takes years for the effects of chemotherapy to disappear. Now it's recovery time. I am on a hormonal medicine for five years; it, too, has its side effects. But I am not letting any of this get in the way.

My last chemotherapy session was on 5 January 2019. Eight months later, I went to VIVAMAYR again, this time with my boy. We had two free days before the results of the blood test arrived. I wanted to use that time to show him the beautiful lake and mountains which had captivated me so much the last time.

As we walked around the valley, I became breathless, something I had noticed in the past month. My head was pounding. We had to take frequent breaks. The one-and-a-half-hour walk took us two hours because of all the stops I made.

That evening I met the doctor. He made me lie down, saw my reports, felt my tummy, and said, 'I don't believe this! Your haemoglobin is barely seven. How are you walking around and being so cheerful?' I said, 'Today I even finished that valley walk.'

He looked at me in disbelief and continued, 'Your overall parameters should have been worse this time, considering you underwent chemotherapy. But they are actually better. And your body is full of vitality.'

This doctor meets hundreds of patients. He couldn't have remembered what he told me last time. But his words were etched in my mind. I had progressed from 'you are a depressed person' to 'your body is full of vitality' in one year despite going through surgery and chemotherapy.

I choked, wanting to cry, but I couldn't let down my guard in front of the hot doctor. So I tried to smirk like John Travolta, thinking my charm would work on him this time. He looked at me blankly, and called out, 'Next.'

Acknowledgements

I want to thank many people, starting from my forefathers and ancestors. The causes they created had my existence as the effect. A big thank you for bringing me into the world. I want to thank my parents, Anita and Yajan, who always underestimated their dorky daughter when it came to dating and sex, and this book is predominantly about that. So, yes, kids are always on a mission to prove their parents wrong. I want to thank my partner of eighteen years, but I don't know if I should be grateful to him or curse him, for at the age of thirty-seven I have spent more than half my life with only one man. I mean, that's good, but other territories must be explored at least before commitment. I am grateful to my kids, Virajveer and Varushka, who have graciously accepted the baton of my legacy, which is to always prove parents wrong and strictly adhere to the unpredictable behaviour associated with this tiny species. I am thankful to my in-laws, Poonam and Virendra, the rock stars who don't mind me dissecting our relationship in this fun space; my brother-in-law, Aparshakti, whose laughter is the best option after Raag Malhar to implore the rain gods; and my sister-in-law, Aakriti, who is forever my sounding board. I am so fortunate to have you all in my life. My friends, who are like family and without whom I wouldn't have tried the death-defying stunts mentioned in the book – thank you for always having my back and front and being the reason for the guts that I managed to muster in the few drunk nights we had. I also want to thank Chiki, my publisher. You, my friend, are the only one to know, apart from my make-out routine (since no moment of my life has been spared a discussion, followed by you texting me for more details, of course, for the book) the OCD that I have with underwear – they are all the same colour. I haven't mentioned the colour in the book; it's a special bond between Chiki and me!

I am also grateful to the entire team at Juggernaut and the Zoom calls we had because of which I associate some of you either with a frozen smile, a blank video, an echoing voice or the omnipresent Pinky, your help who always makes it a point to dust, sweep and clean your laptop screen with Colin while you are still on a call – the pleasures of making a project happen during lockdown.

A Note on the Author

Tahira Kashyap Khurrana is a writer and film-maker based in Mumbai. She is the author of three books and has directed two acclaimed short films, *Pinni* and *Toffee*.

juggernaut

THE APP
FOR INDIAN
READERS

*Fresh, original books tailored for
mobile and for India. Starting at ₹10.*

juggernaut.in

1

CRAFTED
FOR MOBILE
READING

Thought you would never read a book
on mobile? Let us prove you wrong.

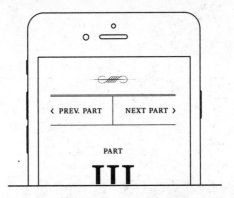

Beautiful Typography

The quality of print transferred
to your mobile. Forget ugly PDFs.

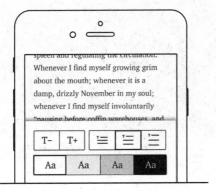

Customizable Reading

Read in the font size, spacing
and background of your liking.

AN EXTENSIVE LIBRARY

Including fresh, new, original Juggernaut books from the likes of Sunny Leone, Praveen Swami, Husain Haqqani, Umera Ahmed, Rujuta Diwekar and lots more. Plus, books from partner publishers and loads of free classics. Whichever genre you like, there's a book waiting for you.

DON'T JUST READ; INTERACT

We're changing the reading experience from passive to active.

Ask authors questions

Get all your answers from the horse's mouth.
Juggernaut authors actually reply to every
question they can.

Rate and review

Let everyone know of your favourite reads or
critique the finer points of a book – you will be
heard in a community of like-minded readers.

Gift books to friends

For a book-lover, there's no nicer gift than
a book personally picked. You can even
do it anonymously if you like.

Enjoy new book formats

Discover serials released in parts over
time, picture books including comics,
and story-bundles at discounted rates.
And coming soon, audiobooks.

4

LOWEST PRICES & ONE-TAP BUYING

Books start at ₹10 with regular discounts and free previews.

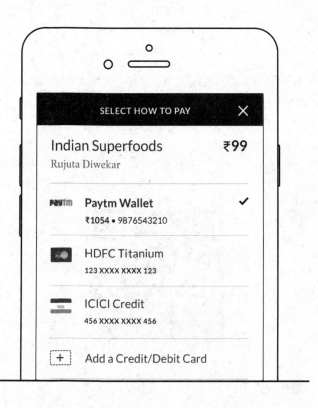

Paytm Wallet, Cards & Apple Payments

On Android, just add a Paytm Wallet once and buy any book with one tap. On iOS, pay with one tap with your iTunes-linked debit/credit card.

Click the QR Code with a QR scanner app
or type the link into the Internet browser
on your phone to download the app.

For our complete catalogue, visit www.juggernaut.in
To submit your book, send a synopsis and two
sample chapters to books@juggernaut.in
For all other queries, write to contact@juggernaut.in